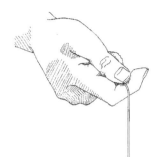

Pendulum, L-Rod, Y-Rod
The Ultimate Guide to Dowsing

By Barbara Dowdy-Trabke, M.H.

Copyright (c) 2007 ETC Publishing

Published by ETC Publishing
Printed in the United States of America.

ISBN 978-1-930038-27-1

For requests and inquiries contact:
ETC Publishing Reno, NV;
www.etcpublishing.com

First Edition, First Printing 2007

Cover Design by Gary Dunham

Illustrations by Rachelle Dowdy

Concepts presented in this book derive from traditional European and American metaphysical and folk lore. They are not to be understood as directions, recommendations or prescriptions of any kind. Nor does the author or publisher make any claim to do more than provide information and report this lore.

Library of Congress Cataloging-in-Publication Data

Dowdy-Trabke, Barbara.
  Pendulum, L-Rod, Y-Rod : the ultimate guide to dowsing / by Barbara Dowdy-Trabke. -- 1st ed.
    p. cm.
  Includes index.
  ISBN-13: 978-1-930038-27-1 (91695 : alk. paper)
  1. Dowsing. I. Title.
  BF1628.D69 2007
  133.3'23--dc22
                                                    2007021495

Dedication

This book is dedicated to Charles Lasater, Asa Dowdy, Jr., Raymon Grace, Walt Woods and Bill Askin, the five people who most influenced and inspired my dowsing, and ultimately my healing work and spiritual quest.

Contents

Pendulum, L-Rod, Y-Rod

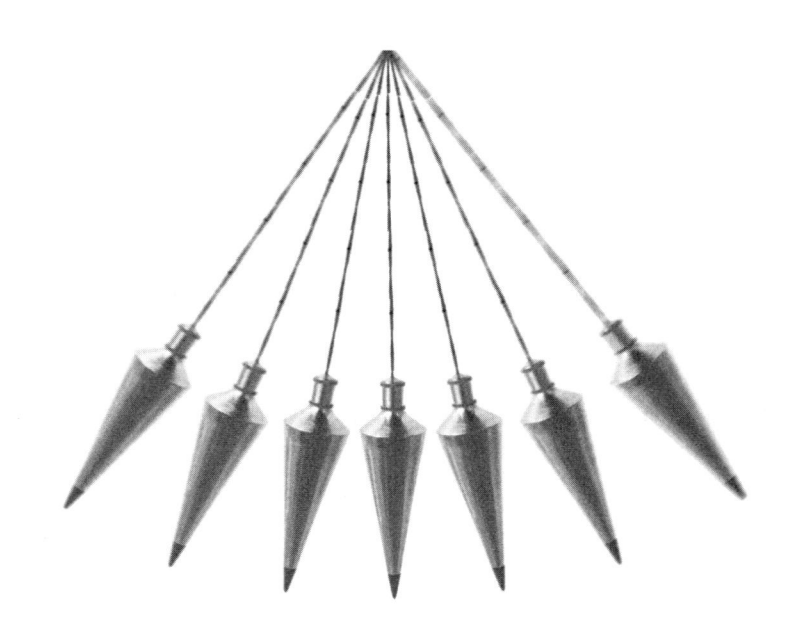

Introduction

Questions, questions, questions! We all have questions and face decisions every day of our lives. What do we do when we need answers and it seems impossible to find them? What do we do when there seems to be no way to confirm an answer we do come up with? Can we feel confident about our decisions? Or, how can we be sure we have based our decisions on the correct information?

When answers are needed, a pendulum is a remarkable tool; the ability to use a pendulum is a skill worth acquiring! In this book I will share with you the techniques for using the pendulum and other dowsing instruments. I have been working with these tools for many years now, and for me the when, where, and how to use the tools we will talk about is as natural as breathing. It feels as though this skill has been programmed into my psyche.

In this book I will explore a variety of methods and techniques with you, so that you can gain access to the flow of energy that surrounds all of us, and begin to find your own answers to the questions you have. Follow the simple, accurate methods I have used and taught for many years, and you can feel confident that you will be able to find the answers to your many questions. Using the pendulum can become as natural as breathing for you, too.

The techniques I will demonstrate in this book have been engraved in my being for so many years that I use my pendulum naturally and process the information instinctively. Use them regularly, and you too will feel confident of your skill.

Whether you use a pendulum, L-Rod, Y-Rod, or bobber, technically this is known as **dowsing**. One can dowse for water, for minerals, for lost objects, for information, for confirming an answer—endless possibilities.

The pendulum has some of the same uses as the other dowsing instruments; however, each had its own unique qualities. The pendulum has the advantage of being easier to carry in a pocket or in a purse; one can hold it in one hand, leaving the other free. I often use my pendulum to find out if someone will like a certain gift, even how much (to what degree or percent) they will like it. I might ask "Is this watermelon ripe?" "Where is the best place to go for vacation?" "What price should I sell my home for?" Or, I might use the pendulum to gain a clearer understanding from a Tarot card spread.

I prefer using my pendulum when I map-dowse for water, or to discover whether or not the soul of someone who has died crossed over (and if not, later, after helping them cross over, my pendulum can be used to confirm they have completed their journey). Many people use their pendulum to check to see if they need to be taking certain vitamin or herbal supplements, to confirm which ones are best for them, to ascertain how many capsules should be taken and how often.

Any list of reasons we can compile for using a pendulum certainly runs the gamut of daily living experiences and then some! In short, any time you have a question, you can use the pendulum or one of the other dowsing tools to get an answer. This is not magic, not a ouija board. In this book I will show you how to make sure that your pendulum, L-Rod, or Y-Rod is programmed, so that you never feel any reason to fear the process or the answers you discover as you work with these tools.

How accurate is the pendulum? Every person who uses one has their own answer to this question, and no one can argue with another's perception of their outcome. But, if you absorb the information I'm going to share with you, believe in it, program your pendulum correctly, and use it, use it, use it, there is no reason not to experience nearly 100% accuracy!

Do I use the pendulum every day? Probably. I have been known to whip out the pendulum at a moment's notice. For me, using these tools has become as natural as breathing. In short, I have "become the pendulum"—a technique you too can learn, and which I will explain later in the book.

Everyone can learn the techniques I'll share with you in these pages. Believe that you can learn them and you will. Henry Ford said it very well, "If you believe you can do something or believe you can't, you're probably right."

This ultimate guide to dowsing will reveal how to successfully use pendulums, L-Rods, and Y-Rods. It will offer a wide perspective on how others successfully have used these tools (including their backgrounds and stories). You will also find a variety of techniques and suggestions you can apply in your own research and discovery process—in short, everything that you need to use your pendulum successfully.

The belief part, well, that's up to you!

"Life is an adventurous journey meant to be lived to the fullest. Every day should be filled with learning, laughter, joy, and love, living in daily communion with our Creator."

Barbara Dowdy-Trabke

EPREUVE *par la* BAGUETTE.

Chapter 1

How Does Dowsing Work?

Everyone who is new to using the pendulum (or doing any other type of dowsing or energy work for that matter), is curious to understand how it works. Personally, I probably understand less how it works than how to work it. Using the pendulum is a matter of using energy.

Energy is all around us. Each of us is surrounded by our own, individual energy field, called our **aura**. There are seven layers to our aura. The first layer is white, and in most people only extends about an inch outside their body. The second layer extends several inches, and the third goes out several feet. The second and third layers are colored. The basic colors of the auras of every living being are the same as the colors of the rainbow. However, when we are sick, dying, angry, upset, deceitful or in other unhealthy states of physical, mental, and spiritual being, we can have black, brown, grey, sparks, and other murky colors and configurations in our aura. The aura truly reflects the energy of what we are thinking, feeling, and being.

Other energy layers of our aura can extend out many feet, yards, and even miles, if we work to have this happen, and then can be pulled in very close if we feel we need to protect ourselves and our privacy. Our aura extends out and around us not only front, back, and to the sides, but also up and down. We are each encapsulated in a sphere of auric energy.

I believe one reason dowers are able to find water using their dowsing tools is because our aura extends well into the earth and down into the depths where water is found. In a very spiritual and not easily explicable way, a dowser "tunes in" to the energy of the earth and the water streams that run through it. The dowser's energy field *feels* the energy of water coursing beneath the surface of the earth.

There are seven major **chakras** or *energy centers* in our body. The energy centers also correspond to the colors of the rainbow. The first center extends from our perineum, and is known as the base (or root) chakra; the color is red. The second is the pelvic (or sacral) chakra, located about four inches below the navel; the color is orange. The third chakra is the solar plexus, at the stomach; the color is yellow. The fourth is the heart chakra; the color is green. The fifth is the throat chakra; the color is blue. The sixth is the third eye, in the center of the forehead, just above and between the eyes; the color is indigo. The seventh is the crown chakra, extending from the top of our head; the color is violet, and as this chakra rises above us, the color becomes white.

The base and the crown chakra become a portal for energy running up and down through our body. The second through the sixth chakras exist not only in the front of our body, but go through our body and extend out the back. Many healers, when working with a person's energy via their chakra system, check only the front chakras and forget that the chakras extending from the back of the body are also very important. If one or more of the front chakras need healing or balancing, quite often the corresponding back chakra will need work as well.

Besides these seven major chakras, we also have several minor chakras in our hands and in our feet. If you have ever worked with a healer, you may have noticed how warm their hands are. This is because of the tremendous amount of heat and energy coming out of the minor chakras in their hands.

To be able to comprehend how dowsing works, it is important to understand these basics of auric and energy patterns, because it is energy that makes our body work, just as it is energy that makes the pendulum work. Energy is what makes all dowsing work. By now, you certainly understand that each of us, in fact, **are** energy. When all of our energy leaves our body, we will cease to exist (we will be dead).

Have you ever noticed that sick people or very old people, or people full of disease, are low on energy? That's why adding a supplement of absorbable minerals will give them more energy. The additional minerals cause more electrical magnetic energy in their body. When we love ourselves, take care of ourselves, eat well, drink lots of pure water, get plenty of sleep and rest, are strong, healthy, and full of life, we can feel the energy in our bodies. If the opposite is true, we feel drained and tired—a state of being typified by the lack of energy, or the lack of good health.

While the previous paragraphs have explored some of the physical manifestations and expressions of energy in our physical body, it is important to understand that energy is all around us. After a rain storm, for instance, you can see a bit of the energy of the earth when you catch a glimpse of a rainbow. The earth has been washed clean, the rain drops project the prism of color we can see. Have you ever noticed that the colors of a rainbow are red, orange, yellow, green, blue, violet, and white—just the same colors of our chakras, and in the same order?

Be aware there is that which is known as *light energy,* sometimes called "good energy" or "positive energy"; and there is also *dark energy,* sometimes called "negative energy". We use the term *dark/negative energy* to define an experience where dark forces come into play. Later in this book I will explain how to protect yourself from negative energy when you are dowsing.

Now, dowsing is not a form of voodoo; it is not the ouija board. When we use the pendulum or do any type of dowsing, it is important to take steps to protect ourselves, and only allow *light/positive energy* or the power of our Creator to be accessed or used. All of this will be ensured when you use the **4-Step Program** explained later in the book.

When we use the pendulum for dowsing, we access the energy of the Creator, our personal energy, **and** the energy that is all around us. Some people are able to tap into this energy more readily, and as a result they are better at using the pendulum than others. Other reasons some people find it easier to work with the dowsing tools, for instance, may be as a result of their level of knowledge, practice, and belief. It is my hope—and the purpose of this book—to make it as easy as possible for you to tap into the energy. I hope that by reading this information, by putting into practice what I explain, and by practicing and making dowsing a part of your life, you too will become a consistent and accurate dowser.

I know that when I dowse, I am using help from our Creator as well as from my Higher Self. I would not be able to get the accurate answers I do if this were not so. I also know that the more pure one can keep their body, the greater the energy flow will be throughout the body; this energy flow is necessary to achieve consistent and accurate dowsing results.

By *"keeping oneself pure"*, I mean keeping all levels of one's being pure: body, mind, and soul. The purer we are, the lighter our energy core is, and the stronger flow of energy we can expect to experience. We basically want to get as close to +50 on the **Negative/Positive Chart** as possible (see page 51). The saying, "Cleanliness is next to Godliness," is not only about keeping our bodies clean, but also our mind and spirit/soul.

The purer we are, the greater and more successful our energy work will be. People who come up with a negative reading on the Negative/Positive Chart will have a hard time doing accurate energy work, i.e., dowsing, using the pendulum, etc. Their core is dark and heavy.

This means that positive energy has a hard time flowing through them. And they tend to attract people of the same ilk.

When any type of energy work is to be done, it must be done with love and for the greater good of all. Should you find yourself testing on the negative side of the chart used for checking character, you have not as yet reached the level of purity needed to do good energy work. That does not mean that you cannot learn to dowse, but you may need to take a variety of steps to clear and brighten your energy field before successfully carrying out dowsing work. (Additionally, a negative reading most likely indicates that you are currently not able to successfully apply your skill to other types of energy work, such as Reiki or similar alternative healing modalities.)

To keep the body pure, we need to be concerned with what we put into our body. We need to drink lots of pure water and eat wholesome food. Just as important is to stay away from processed, energy depleted food, chemicals, additives, strong drink, unnecessary over-the-counter medications, and illegal drugs. Simply put, we should try to keep ourselves as free as possible from all things synthetic, artificial, and processed. In addition, it is a good idea to periodically cleanse the body with liver and gallbladder flushes, parasite, colon, and blood cleansers, and then support or build our body with quality foods, herbal supplements, natural vitamins, and minerals. The added benefit of paying attention to the needs of our body is to help keep us healthy and strong, with extra vim and vigor!

Now keeping our mind clean is important too. We need to be aware, conscious in our choices of what we see or watch, what we read, the language that comes out of our mouth, our actions, the company we keep and the places we go. Make every effort to stay away from places where dark and earthbound spirits dwell, i.e., bars, smoking establishments, and such places.

When you are tempted to indulge in any of the vices, it is easy for earthbound spirits to attach themselves to you. Then you will have to contend with their addictions and dark energy as well as your own weakness. Periodically, we need to have any negative **energy cords** cut. If you do not know how to do this yourself, then you need to find someone who does, and have them perform this simple and quick healing for you.

Tip: *I always use the help of Archangel Michael when I cut negative energy cords; and I always ask that healing take place for all those who were attached to the cords (i.e., the giver of the negative cord as well as the receiver).*

Now for the spiritual aspect of keeping our core pure: one of the most positive things we can do for ourselves is to surround ourselves with positive, loving, spiritual, happy people, and keep our thoughts and emotions positive and elevated. When you create this shift in your life, not only will you notice the difference in how you feel, but other people will notice the changes in you as well.

I am not suggesting that you need to become religious, nor do I want to proselytize you to my religion or way of believing. There are many people on this planet, and we do not all call God by the same name. That is not important. What **is** important is realizing that a Higher Power is at work when we are dowsing. We become plugged into the energy of a Higher Power for the purpose of dowsing.

For example, I have observed on many occasions that people who are not plugged into positive energy for the purpose of dowsing are not able to use a Y-Rod. My experience indicates that the same is in all likelihood true when using the pendulum, because not all people can use the pendulum the first time they try. This is another reason to follow the **4-Step Program** you can find on page 22, and why it is so important to do so. The method is used to cleanse the pendulum, protect you, program the pendulum, plug you in, and demonstrate the correct way to use your pendulum. I know it will work—because I have seen the method work and taught many people how to use the pendulum following the same steps outlined in this book.

All religions encourage us to ask for what we want to receive, and assure us that we will be granted the help and protection we need. So, quite simply, this is what we are going to do: we ask the Creator for help and knowledge, and it is given.

In this and all energy work, the main component is **belief.** That is why we will start with simple questions, and as we gain confidence, we will ask the more complicated ones. As our belief grows, so does our skill.

There will be people who think that using the pendulum (or any type of dowsing tool for that matter) is the work of the devil, that we should not try to know the future. When we use the pendulum, however, we are not trying to tell the future. Foretelling the future is not possible; we all have free choice, so the future is not set in stone. When we dowse or use the pendulum, we are seeking information to help us make the best possible decisions as we prepare for our future.

Business owners and entrepreneurs do much the same thing. They consider all the possibilities and all the variables when coming up with a business plan. It would not be sound business practice if they did not try to get all the information available so that they could make the best possible business decisions.

This is just what you are doing when you use the pendulum. You are trying to get as much information as possible. And if you follow the 4-Step Program outlined in this book, you will be able to gain a great deal of insight, accessing the most accurate information possible—because you will be receiving help from our Creator, your spirit guides, divine beings, and your Higher Self. So, let's get started. There's lots to learn.

Chapter 2

Your Pendulum

A pendulum can be made out of any object that swings freely from a chain, cord or thread. A pendulum should have a touch of weight to it, a bit of a point and be able to be attached with a thread, cord, or small chain. Your pendulum can cost anywhere from pennies to beaucoup bucks.

When I first started, I would sometimes be caught without my pendulum, and even today that will occasionally happen. I have been known to use a paperclip as my pendulum, attaching it to a cord or string in order to use it. On occasion I have had to use a needle and thread—and have discovered that even something this basic can work well. Though neither the paperclip nor the needle has enough weight to be an ideal pendulum, in an emergency we make due.

Sometimes a crystal necklace on a chain can work nicely. Such a piece is often handy just hanging around your neck, ready to use, while adding an attractive accent to whatever you happen to be wearing. Many pendant necklaces will also work well, as long as the pendants are pointed or oval in shape, and have a good swing to them. Square or round pendants do not work too well. In a pinch, let your imagination take over and use whatever is at hand.

I have three favorite pendulums. The first is a metal, pointed, teardrop shape about one inch long with a 6-inch chain; at the opposite end is a little metal goddess shape. This pendulum "lives" in a plastic case inside my purse.

My second pendulum was a birthday gift from a friend and is made of rose quartz. It has a stylized, pointed, teardrop shape and is attached to a 4-inch beaded chain with a small rose quartz teardrop at the opposite end. This one lives in a pop-open plastic pouch on my stand with all of my angel cards, tarot cards, sage, holy water, and such. This rascally little pendulum disappeared once for about 4 months, and then reappeared in the very same spot where it had originally been placed.

My third pendulum is exactly the same as my second—a gift from a friend who felt very badly about the disappearance of the second pendulum. This little guy travels with me, as I can easily slip the pouch into my jeans pocket and away we go.

Tip: *Keeping your pendulum in a pouch protects it from damage as you travel.*

My friends use a variety of objects for pendulums. For instance, Raymon uses a pendulum made from a bullet which he attached to a chain. Tom always uses the same type of rose quartz pendulum as mine. For years, we were in the same dowsing club in Fairbanks, Alaska. Tom is the one who gifted me with my first "good" pendulum, and Donna gave me the second.

Asa is constantly buying light fixture pulls and using these; the weight is a little too heavy for me, but he likes them.

You will find that, in the "perfect" pendulum, weight can be extremely important. You need one that has a bit of weight to it, but is not so heavy that you will be tired from holding it if you are dowsing for any length of time. I once had a wooden pendulum on a cord that could be worn around the neck. It was just too lightweight, so it didn't have the perfect feel or swing to it for me. But it lived on the floor lamp light switch next to my bed, and was very convenient when I wanted to do some late night dowsing. Still, it was no great loss when it slipped to the floor one night, and my dog decided that it made a nice chewy.

I have found that I like the chain length to be between 4 and 6 inches. Even longer chains can work just as well, because you just wrap the extra length around your fingers. Too long a chain, though, just gets in the way, and a chain that is too big around or too heavy isn't ideal. I like a slightly delicate to mildly sturdy pendulum chain—that feels best for me. (And I do tend to like chains better than cords, but that is my own preference.)

So, all that being said, find a pendulum that "speaks" to you. You'll know it when you see it. It will catch your attention and you will be drawn to it. When you pick it up, it will feel "right" in your hand—the balance, the color, the weight, the material it is made from, the look—all of it will appeal to you. You might as well buy it right away, because if you don't, you will mourn the decision for a long, long time. You will probably find yourself out looking for another one just like it, and not be able to find one. The pendulum that was "yours" has been lost to you. Don't let this happen to you.

When you see the pendulum that "has your name on it," give yourself permission to get it. A pendulum is something that can last you a lifetime. One word of caution: *crystals break easily when dropped*. If your crystal should drop and break, it is ruined. So, if you are the klutzy type, a crystal pendulum might not be the right choice for you.

It is very important that your pendulum have the right "swing". Most pendulums that are available for purchase will have the correct feel/swing. However, if you don't want to buy one, you can easily make your own if you are in any way good with your hands. You can often find stones or crystals that are wire wrapped and have a loop at the top so a chain can be attached.

If the swing doesn't feel quite right, often having a slightly larger metal loop on the part that attaches the stone to the chain will help to make a better swing. Some people like to decorate the chain with extra beads, which can be quite attractive. Feel free to be creative. Make something that is pleasing to the eye and pleasing to the touch. It can be very gratifying to have constructed the "perfect" pendulum for your own personal use.

How to hold your pendulum

To use your pendulum, grasp the chain between the thumb and forefinger of your right hand. The chain should be long enough to allow for an approximately 4-inch swing. (If you are left-handed, use your left hand to grasp and swing the pendulum.)

If the cord or chain is too long, I wrap it around my right forefinger to get the excess out of the way, and then I grasp the chain between my thumb and fore-finger (see picture).

There is another way of holding the pendulum, quite similar to the first. Drape the cord over your forefinger, curl the remaining fingers of your hand around the tail of the cord to hold it in place.

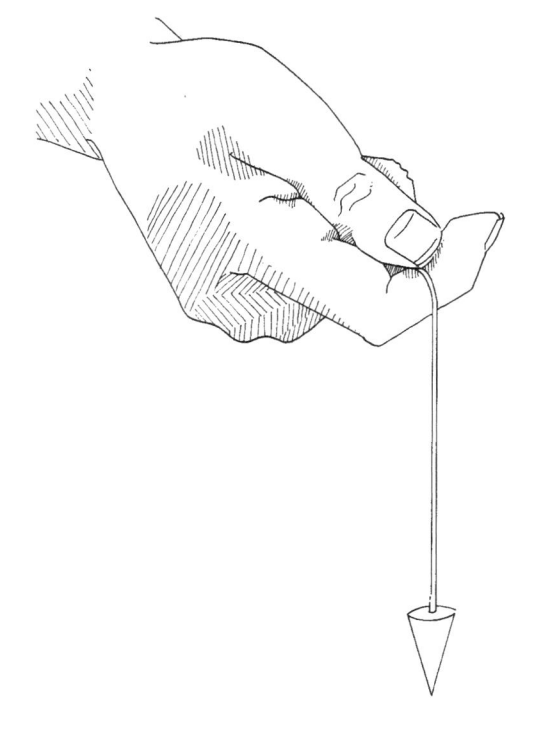

Chapter 3

4-Step Program

This 4-Step Program teaches you to use your pendulum correctly:

First: **Cleanse your pendulum**. After the initial cleansing, cleansing will always be done as needed.

Second: **Surround yourself with the white light of protection before you work with the pendulum.** Learn to surround yourself with *white light* every time you use your pendulum.

Third: **Program yourself and your pendulum**. It is necessary to do this the first time you use your pendulum, whenever you need to change the program, and whenever you find that you have forgotten how to use your pendulum (for instance, due to lack of use or a considerable time lapse between usages).

Fourth: **Following this instruction, use your pendulum often.** This will ensure that you become increasingly skilled with this tool—more confident as you practice, practice, practice!

Step One:

Cleansing your new or existing pendulum

Many people ask if it is all right to allow others to touch their pendulum. My response is, "As far as letting others touch my pendulum, I don't have a problem with my friends touching or holding my pendulum. But then, I know my friends, and they are honest and trustworthy people. Would I let a stranger or someone of dubious character hold my pendulum? That is a different matter entirely." *If you don't know the person well enough to let them drive your car, then you probably don't know them well enough to let them handle your pendulum.*

If you have purchased a new pendulum, never cleansed your existing one, or if someone you don't know (or someone who gives you any doubt or concern) picks up your pendulum, then it is time to immediately cleanse your pendulum. It can be done in several ways using method A, B, C, or D.

A. Place the pendulum in a window where it will get sunlight and moonlight for 24 hours.

B. Submerge the pendulum in sea salt for 24 hours.

C. Wash the pendulum with holy water.

D. Or, the way I prefer, place about ½ inch of sea salt in a small glass bowl, place the pendulum in the salt (or lay pendulum on top of salt). Place the glass bowl with the pendulum on a windowsill to get sunlight and moonlight for 24 hours (or a little more if that's how it works out). Remove the pendulum from the salt and then bless your pendulum with a little holy water sprinkled on it, repeating, "You are now cleansed in the name of the Father, the Son, and the Holy Spirit." Or, "You are now cleansed with the power of our Creator."

After using any of the above-listed methods (or a combination of them all as in the way I do it), your pendulum has been cleansed and is ready for use.

Warning!—*Do not place the metal chain attached to your pendulum in sea salt because if you forget and leave it there for days, over time the chain may become weakened by the salt. After about 8 years of use and cleansing in this manner, my favorite pendulum fell apart and needed to be restrung.*

Regarding the question: "What is the best time of the month for cleansing the pendulum in the moonlight?" I do not worry about the stage of the moon (Full, Waning, Waxing or New Moon), partly because I am not an expert in the moon phases. I carry out a cleansing when needed. If you feel strongly about cleansing only during certain moon phases, then by all means follow your own inclinations. Do not worry if the very time that you choose for pendulum cleansing turns out to be a cloudy night; your cleansing will still work properly. Nighttime is no less night because the sky happens to be cloudy.

My pendulums live a pretty sheltered life (people-touching-wise), and I don't have to cleanse them very often because I always work surrounded by a white light of protection. However, if I were teaching a class with them, or was in any way concerned about who may have had contact with them, then I would cleanse the pendulums.

And always, always, always cleanse a pendulum you have just purchased or received as a gift *before* you ever use it. Basically, while you know who gave it to you and their energy may be perfectly fine, you don't know who has touched the pendulum prior to it being purchased

(or where it has been on its journey to you). This is just good common sense.

It is not a good idea, of course, to make the person who gave you the pendulum as a gift feel uncomfortable or unappreciated by immediately cleansing it in their presence. Of course not! Hold it, caress it, enjoy it, love it, and ooh and ah to your hearts content. Then when you are home alone, make sure that you cleanse your pendulum so that no traces of negative energy or dark influence are upon it.

Step Two: Protection and preparation

It is very important to set parameters before you start dowsing. This is to protect yourself from undue influences, to shield yourself from any harm or negativity. Setting parameters will ultimately help your dowsing to be more accurate. Dowsing is not like using a ouija board. It is often said that when people use a ouija board, both good and bad influences from the spirit realm can come into the space. This is not what happens or what you can expect when you use a pendulum following the 4-Step Program, because we always protect ourselves first. The pendulum works differently for us because we program the pendulum to work differently. It is important that you use the following prayer (or formula, if you prefer to think of it this way) **each and every time** at the beginning of dowsing.

This formula will protect you and improve the accuracy of your dowsing. The prayer is best repeated every time you pick up your pendulum, until it becomes an automatic part of your process. If you practice dowsing every day, it will take only a few weeks before it is automatic.

When you finally achieve automatic pilot, simply the act of picking up the pendulum and holding it in the dowsing position with the intent to dowse, will place protection around you and any others that are involved in the dowsing that you are preparing to do.

Here is the protection exercise and prayer:

1. **Ground yourself:** Close your eyes briefly and imagine your feet on the floor or imagine the earth beneath you. Feel your connection to your physical body and your physical reality.

2. **Surround yourself with white light:** Imagine yourself standing or sitting in a bright and light space or in the sunlight, with white light all around you.

3. **Say the following**:

"Dearest Lord, guardian angels, spirit guides: I ask your protection as I do this work. Surround me and protect me with white light. Do not allow any harm to come to me or to others; do not allow me to be negatively influenced as I do this work. May the information come from only the highest source. Do not allow any evil or dark influences to be part of this work I am doing.

"May this information that I receive be 100% accurate and may it be used for the best interest and highest good of all. I thank you for your love, help, and support."

The above prayer/formula will not only protect you but will help to make your dowsing more accurate. And no matter how you look at it, why would you want to dowse if you are not going to be accurate? *Completely following these steps each and every time before you dowse is as important as the dowsing itself.*

Before long, all you will even have to do is pick up the pendulum and sense the grounding; feel the white light surrounding and swirling around you; silently or out loud mention the name of our Lord or the Creator who is the source of your belief system; think of your own guardian angels and spirit guides; and think protection, love, and accurate information. All the protection you need will be in place!

Tip: *Protection/prayer must be done every time until it is automatic. It only becomes automatic with practice, practice, practice!*

Any type of energy work, of which dowsing is a part, should only be done in love, and with the light and energy of our Creator. This will keep integrity in place. If the work is done in love, greed will not have a chance to take over. If the work is done in pure love, it will be done to the greater good of all concerned. This needs to be part of our preparation for dowsing and all forms of energy work.

Breathing and breath work is also very important. Your breathing should be slow, quiet, and regular. This will help to put you in the *energy zone.* Any other type of breathing (fast, loud, irregular, pained, wheezing, etc.) will keep you distracted, unable to focus.

I cannot emphasize too strongly just how important all of this is (the protection, working in a state of love, breathing slowly and regularly) to successful dowsing.

Step Three:

Program yourself to use the pendulum

The third step involves programming yourself. This **Basic Program** will then work for any pendulum or other dowsing instrument (such as: L-Rod, Y-Rod, or bobber) you pick up and use.

Programming is done only once unless and until you need to make temporary changes. Then you perform the programming step as needed. Now if, for whatever reason, you do not use your pendulum for a year or two, I would suggest reprogramming again to refresh yourself, so that you know just what you are doing.

Caution!—If you do not know how to use a pendulum to get a *Yes* or *No* answer, you must at this point proceed to *Step Four: Learning to use the pendulum (see page 30)*. Read the first ten paragraphs in that section, and follow directions until you come to the four ****'s. You will then be able to come back and complete the Basic Program from this point. **Do not continue** until you read Step Four, understand how to use the pendulum, and practice using the pendulum. The reason is, you will be using the pendulum as you go through *Step Three: Program yourself to use the pendulum*.

Basic Program

1) Obtain permission: To obtain permission to continue, hold your pendulum as you ask: *"May I, Can I, Should I?"* When you receive a *Yes* response, continue. (If you are unsure at all of the purpose for this step, you will find the explanation in greater depth a little further along in this book.)

2) Begin program: Input the following program by reading it silently or aloud:

Primary Program: which will be continually in effect until I choose to make changes.

Covers all dowsing requests and responses.

The purpose is to find answers, determine amounts, effects, conditions, circumstances, influences, times, measurements, distances, numbers, percentages, and other requested areas.

Dowsing communication is to be inter-cooperative and restricted to: The Overall, Universal Superconscious (God, I Am, The Creator, Abba Father, The Great Spirit), my Superconscious, my Higher Self and approved Spirit Guides, Guardian Angels, and other divine helpers, my Mind Systems, my Subconscious and its related systems. This is to cause me or others no harm, discomfort, pain or loss of energy, either physically or spiritually.

Influences such as misleading thoughts, imaging, wishes, or any other conditions from any source, physical or non-physical, including my own or other persons, entities or mind systems of any kind are not to take control in any way, and are not to affect me adversely or cause incorrect dowsing answers.

Time, as related to dowsing, is to be in my time unless otherwise requested.

Answers are to be selected from all available knowledge and information sources as long as they fall into the above-stated divine help.

The method of answering by the pendulum is to be:

1) Swing to *Ready for question* position.

2) Swing to *Yes, No,* or *other appropriate position* to indicate the most appropriate answer for the question asked.

3) *Clockwise spin* for searching for an answer. If clockwise spin continues, this indicates waiting or working on a problem or question. Clockwise spin can also show the direction of the flow of energy in a particular situation.

4) *Counterclockwise spin* for removing negative influences, negative energy, or any other unwanted things. Counterclockwise can also show the direction of the flow of energy in a particular situation.

Temporary changes may be made by me while dowsing, reverting back to this primary program after use.

Program changes like adding, deleting, or changing may be made by me but only after going through the complete primary program.

End of program. Thank you.

3) Final check: Ask the dowsing system, "Are the conditions (or changes) acceptable as presented, being clear and non-contradictory, and open to my request?" Do so now with your pendulum. If **Yes**, say, "Thank You." And you are finished.

This process need only be done again if you need to change or add anything to the program, or if you feel that you have forgotten the information because of lack of use or time lapse.

If the answer is **No,** you may have done something wrong and you need to do it again; or the time or place may not be right, so do it at a later time; or you may have been rushed and need to pick a time when you can be more relaxed, when there are fewer distractions.

I will repeat: **when you set this program into place you are programming *yourself* to use the pendulum.** If you were only programming the pendulum, you would have to repeat these steps with every pendulum you used! Steps 1, 2, and 3 must be done before you *ever* pick up your first pendulum and try to use it.

Warning! *You may have been dowsing for many years, but if you have not input this 4-Step Program, it must be done so that your dowsing is accurate, and you are protected.*

Once these steps have been completed, you can safely and accurately pick up any pendulum and it will work just as accurately as the next. That is why a needle on a thread will be just as accurate as the most expensive crystal pendulum you can find.

Most of us just feel more comfortable using our own favorite pendulum over and over again, as we tend to establish comfortable routines. We are all creatures of habit.

If you are familiar with pendulum usage or with dowsing, then everything we have explored so far will probably make sense to you at this point. But if all of this is "as clear as mud" at this point, try reading the whole book before you start the 4-Step Program. If none of this makes any sense after reading the book and going through all the steps, then you are probably just like

me, and learn best when you have a hands-on teacher, taking you by the hand and explaining everything face-to-face, step-by-step.

That's when you call me and arrange a seminar. I'll come and teach you everything you've ever wanted to know about the pendulum and about dowsing.

But, for now, read on! We're just getting started.

Step Four: Learning to use the pendulum

Now for the fun part, step number four. This is where we will pick up the pendulum and actually learn how to use it.

Being right handed, I hold the pendulum in my right hand between my thumb and forefinger. I like to have about 3 to 4 inches of chain hanging down so that I can have a good swing (see diagram on page 21). Shorter than that, and the arc of the pendulum doesn't feel right for me; longer, and I have to hold my hand and arm up too high.

If you are using a necklace or a pendulum with a long chain, you can wrap the chain around your forefinger several times, and then pinch the chain between your thumb and forefinger. (This will get some of the extra chain out of the way.) Here is yet another way of holding the pendulum: I drape the cord over my forefinger; then the cord is held in place by the fingers of my hand being curled in, holding the tail of the cord.

If you are left handed, follow those same directions, using your left hand. If you are ambidextrous, you can use whichever hand feels the most comfortable.

Directions to the pendulum can be given out loud, or given silently in your thoughts. When you first start out, it is best to do all commands verbally, and with a commanding voice. Once comfortable and confident, silent commands work very well.

Holding the pendulum ready for use above **Learning Chart A** (see page 32), ask the pendulum to give you a *Yes* answer. The pendulum will swing up and down, just the way you nod your head "Yes". Many people can accomplish this immediately. Where there is doubt, it will take a little longer. Just continue to hold the pendulum properly, repeat out loud, with a commanding voice: "Give me a *Yes!*"

After a try or two (don't give up), the pendulum will swing up and down, or in a North-South direction. If it doesn't, take your other hand and *make* the pendulum swing. Keep trying till you easily get a *Yes* swing.

Tip: *If you are having a hard time getting the pendulum to swing, there are usually two main reasons for this problem: One has to do with belief. You may just not believe that such a thing is possible, and your subconscious continues to block the process. You may never be able to dowse. Or, you may have been told that dowsing is an evil thing and should be avoided. Until your belief system has changed, you will not be able to use the pendulum or dowse in any way. The second reason for problems getting the pendulum to swing may be that you need to go through* Step Two: Protection,

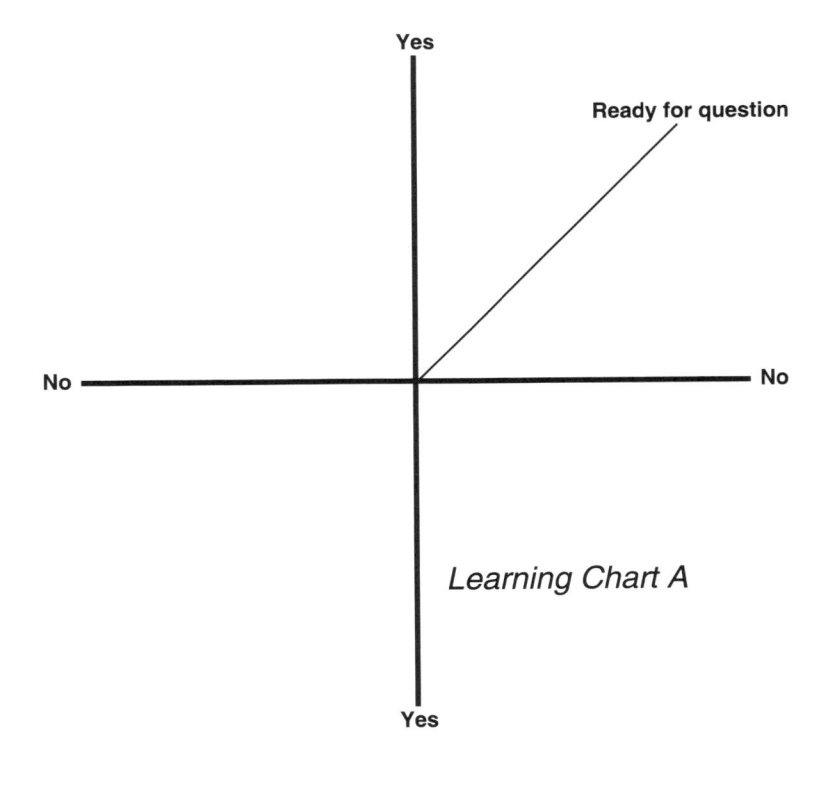

Learning Chart A

one more time. *Once again, this has to do with belief; you must feel fully protected before you will be allowed to receive this gift. (And I do believe that the ability to use the pendulum is a gift from the Divine!)*

Next, ask the pendulum to give you a **No** answer. The pendulum will swing back and forth or crosswise, just the way we turn or shake our head when we indicate "No". Lest we be confused, this is in an East-West direction.

Keep trying until you can get the pendulum to swing properly for **Yes** and for **No**. This is known as training the pendulum. Once you can do this you are finally ready to start using the pendulum. **** (You may now need to go back to *Step Three* of the *Basic Program* on page 27—*Program yourself...*)

Now, knowing that it is possible to influence the movement of the pendulum with your mind or your thoughts, you must practice *taking yourself out of the picture*. If you continue practicing your new ability to influence the movement of the pendulum, you will not be able to achieve accurate dowsing results.

Separate yourself from any particular concern about the outcome of your question, and maintain a curious mindset. Be curious about the answer, rather than certain of it. (Indeed, if receiving accurate answers is not your goal, why even dowse?)

This is where training, experience, and integrity come into play. Just as you want to be able to trust your spiritual advisor, your doctor, your legal advisor, your financial institutions, etc., you will want to be able to trust your dowser, and also yourself as a dowser. So, when it comes to trusting yourself, just look back at the *Primary Program* that you just installed into your little computer brain, and you will realize that you have programmed yourself for accuracy.

So, take yourself out of the emotional picture when you do dowsing, and your answers will be accurate. In other words, don't take it personally. If you can't do that (and I will admit that sometimes it is easier said than done) when you are dowsing for yourself on personal issues, have someone that you trust do the dowsing for you. They won't have a stake in the outcome, so there should be no need for them to influence the pendulum.

The next position on the Learning Chart (on page 32) is **Ready for question.** When you state: "May I, Can I, Should I ask about_____.", and the pendulum swings to *Ready for question*, this means that you have permission to ask about whatever the issue is that you just stated. If you don't get a *Ready for question* indication then—for whatever reason—you do not have permission. **Do not proceed!**

There is a reason. Maybe it isn't the right time to ask. Maybe the universe is not ready for you to have the information. Maybe you don't have all the background data you need, and so the answer will not be accurate. Maybe whatever information you are seeking is none of your business. There are a lot of maybe's... Just know that if you do not get the permission to go on, then don't. You can always try later, and see if you get permission then.

When we dowse, we must respect the boundaries of others. You will need permission when you dowse for a second party. (However, when someone asks you to do dowsing for them, this means that you have their permission.)

You might run into a kind of "murky" zone on occasion. What if a second party asks you to dowse for a third party? You must have that third party's permission, unless it is a minor child, and that child is not yet old enough to give their consent and understand what they are doing; or unless this third party is unable to give permission.

In such an instance I use the phrase: **"For the good of all concerned."** Then, if it is not for the person's good, you won't get the *Yes* or the *Ready for question* go-ahead-indication when you ask, "May I, Can I, Should I."

In the Basic Program under Step One we mentioned *May I, Can I, Should I*. Now you need to understand the importance of the *May I, Can I, Should I*. This question is all about asking permission.

Just as we asked permission to input the Basic Program into our being, we must ask this same permission every time we begin to dowse a new issue. **This is vitally important!**

Tip: May I, Can I, Should I *must be asked/stated every time we begin to dowse a different issue.*

May I is asking if I should do this. It is getting permission. *Can I* is asking if I have the ability to do this. Do I have the skill and all the information I need to be able to get an accurate answer? *Should I* is asking if this is any of my business. Do I, or whomever I am dowsing for, need or have the right to know the answer?

If you don't ask *May I, Can I, Should I*, the pendulum is not going to swing to the *Ready for question* position.

When you are finished dowsing, always end with **"Thank You"**. With these two words, you are thanking the Creator, the Higher Spiritual realm, your Spirit Guides, your Guardian Angels, and your Higher Self for the help that was given. *Thank You* lets all know that you are now finished at this time, and that you appreciate the help given to you. It will also help to insure that the next time you need to use the pendulum, they will be there immediately to offer assistance.

Chapter 4

Ask Specific Questions

When you ask a question, be very specific. Vague questions will get an indecisive answer. Examples: "Will it rain today?" Off the chart vague! Of course it will be raining somewhere in the world today. Will it rain today in Reno?" Even that is too vague. After living in Reno for three years, I know that it can rain in one part of Reno, snow in another, and have the sun shine in still another part of town—all at the same time. "Will it rain a discernible amount today at Butterfly Court in Reno, Nevada?" Now we are getting specific.

"Will it be cold today?" Cold is a relative term. After living 35 years in Fairbanks, Alaska, my idea of cold is not the same as most other people's idea of cold. "Will the temperature hit -35 degrees F today at my home in Fairbanks, Alaska?" Now we are being specific. We stated just how cold and the exact location in Fairbanks. (Exact location is important because the temperature can vary 20 degrees in Fairbanks, depending on location.) You could even get more specific and state the time of day you are asking about.

Here is a case in point regarding just how important it is to be very specific in asking questions when using the pendulum. My friend Diane had been using a certain medication for some time. When she went in for a refill, the pharmacy was out of stock for that item, but the pharmacist recommended a generic brand which he said was just the same.

Diane took the new medication for a short time and soon developed a severe case of edema. Her feet and legs swelled up considerably, as did much of her body, to the point that she was having a hard time getting around. Diane figured that it was probably one of her medications that was causing the problem, and she needed to figure out which one. She had just learned about using the pendulum to differentiate information, and decided to give it a try. The pendulum indicated that the new medication was the culprit. She asked if she needed the medication and the answer was **Yes.**

She was puzzled. How could she need the medication and it still be bad for her? After all, she had been taking the medication for some time, except that now it was the generic brand; yet the pharmacist had told her it was the same. So, she decided to ask if it was the formulation that was causing the problem. The answer to that specific question came back **Yes.**

She decided to call the pharmacist regarding the problem, and was told that the formulation of the generic brand was indeed different from the prescription she had been on previously for some time. Since the first product was now back in stock, she immediately switched back to her former prescription, and within 38 hours the edema was gone. Using the pendulum helped Diane figure out the problem, but only after she was able to ask the specific question correctly.

Sometimes to be specific and to get an accurate answer, you need to ask, "To what degree will something be effective, or to what degree will something be liked." "Will my friend like this sweater?" What friend? What sweater? There may be a dozen sweaters in front of you to choose from. We are not being specific enough. The friend's name should be stated, sometimes even first and last name. (After all, you may have three friends name Marilyn. Which one is it?) Touch the sweater, or in some way indicate which one you are considering.

When finding out if someone would like something, I go by degrees. This is when I use the **Percentage Chart** that you will find on page 43. If someone would like something just a little bit, the Percentage Chart might only indicate they 5% like it. That's a big difference from someone liking it 100%! So I will always ask, "To what degree would she like it?" Now I'm getting a percentage, and I'll be able to make a much better decision.

I often use phrases like *"All things being equal"* and *"For the greater good of all concerned."* You want to give as much information as possible when asking questions, and you should be concerned enough that you look at the whole picture; don't just be self-centered, concerned only with you own interests when asking questions.

In fact, the best way to obtain correct information is by being totally unbiased. Try to remain neutral. Disconnect yourself. If the question concerns you deeply and you cannot keep yourself detached from the outcome, you must ask someone else whom you trust to do the dowsing for you.

I am often requested to dowse information for someone who has a personal stake in the outcome or the answer. It is possible for a person to sway the outcome through the power of their own desires and feelings on a subject. When that happens it is much better to let someone else, who does not have a personal stake in the outcome, do the dowsing for you.

If the question being dowsed concerns another person, it's a good idea to use the person's name when you ask the question because then there is no doubt about who you have in mind (for instance, you may have several granddaughters, more than one neighbor, numerous co-workers, etc.) If it is possible there might still be doubt, you can even get more specific and state the person's address or other information that leaves no doubt about whom you speak.

Tip: *I am often asked to dowse for other people. I have found it very useful, when dowsing for them, to clearly state: "Dowsing for _____, May I, Can I, Should I ask regarding _____?"*

Now ask a simple question. For example, I might ask "May I, Can I, Should I ask about birthday presents for my granddaughter (child's name)?" After getting a **Yes**, the pendulum should swing to the right—to the **Ready for question** position. Then I can ask, "Will (child's name) like this book I'm holding as a birthday present?" If I receive an up/down swing, I have my **Yes** answer. If I get a right/left swing, I have been given a **No** answer.

The following has happened to me and to others. I get a **No** answer, and yet I know that the person I am asking about has an interest in the type of book I have picked out, and that they would just love reading it. So, why did I get a **No**? It could be that they already own the book or they have already read it. Trust your answer. I use this technique almost every time I buy a gift for someone. Remember, the answer is in our time (otherwise known as *real time*), and they may actually purchase the very same thing after you have purchased their gift, but before you plan to give it to them.

So here is another important lesson. Nothing is written in stone. Time rolls on, events bring change, and when asking a question about a possible event in the future, on separate occasions we may get different answers because the equation has changed. So, timing is everything. If you ask the birthday question eleven months before you give the gift, you may get a different answer than you would get if you asked the question just a few days before the birthday.

Being consistent is very important. I am a creature of habit, so consistency is pretty easy for me. When you find what works best for you, continue doing it the same way. Continue asking questions in the same way. The up and down swing is always **Yes**, and the across swing is always **No**. Use the charts in the same manner. When you do something one way one time, and another way another time, you will have problems getting correct answers. Learning the correct way from a great teacher, implementing the 4-Step Program, being non-judgmental/neutral in the dowsing process, belief, practice, and consistency are six of the most important factors in being accurate.

I suggest that you keep a log of your dowsing; purchase a nice ledger just for this purpose. This will let you know just how accurate you are when the future plays itself out. Since most people feel they don't have a lot of time for record-keeping, you may decide not to record the little, insignificant questions and the practice dowsing; but you might keep a log of the important things.

Tip: *I keep a log of my dowsing for wells. That way when the person calls me back after the well is in, I can jot the well statistics down in my book, and I'll have a record of how accurate I am.*

Just to reiterate, so that you know how to properly phrase a question, when you ask: "May I, Can I, Should I ask about_____?", and then get your *Ready for question* response, you will have asked a general question.

When you ask the more specific questions that follow, and in order to elicit a clear **Yes** or **No** answer, you must ask very specific questions.

Here is an example of using the pendulum to query about investments: First we will get permission by asking, "May I, Can I, Should I ask about investments?" Then you get the *Ready for question* indications. Next we will ask our specific questions.

"Is this a good time to buy gold?" Too general.

"Is this a good time for me to buy gold?" Better.

Is this a good time for me to buy Gold Krugerrands, if the price of gold is going to increase in the future?" Much better.

"Is this a good day to buy precious metal mutual funds?" Too general.

"Is this a good day for me to buy precious metal mutual funds?" Better, but get more specific if you can.

Can you see how these questions are different? We need to be **very specific** when asking questions, so that we can get very accurate answers.

With questions like those just mentioned, you will need to use the **Learning Chart B** on page 41, which includes the response: *Maybe/Need more information.* (This response is shown with a backward 45-degree swing.) When you get the *Maybe/Need more information* response to a question, this indicates that there may or may not be a **Yes** or **No** answer to your question—depending on your specific case, or on the parameters that are set. You may need to verbally indicate these parameters, i.e., "for a short term investment", "for a long term investment", "because I will feel more secure owning gold", etc. Or, you may need to do much more research, and know a great deal more about the volatile stock market, before posing the question.

When getting a *Maybe/Need more information* response, the pendulum will swing from *Ready for question* backwards, or counter-clockwise to the *Maybe/ Need more information* mark. If it is not a clearly obvious swing, then you will need to ask whether the answer you are getting is a *Maybe*, or if the correct answer is *Need more information*. That answer, indicated by a **Yes**, provides you with the correct response to your question.

Remember, like computers: "garbage in, garbage out"! If you want your dowsing to be correct, you must learn to phrase your questions properly; and you need to have proper knowledge about the subject that you are dowsing.

Now, let's do some more practice. Here are a few questions you might want to ask. They will be ones in which you have no personal stake, and the outcome won't be that costly if you're not right in the beginning. When you're at the grocery store or at the market, dowse for which watermelon in the case will be the best tasting one. Buy it, take

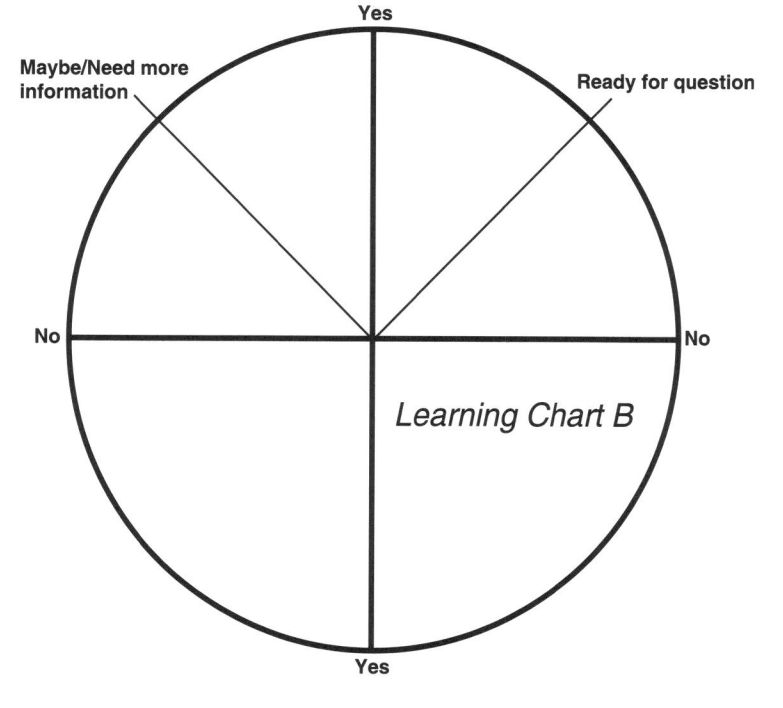

it home, chill it in the refrigerator, and then give it the ole' taste test. Dowse for if the strawberries are sweet and tasty. Dowse to see if the asparagus is young and tender. Dowse to see if this is a good day to take your car to the shop to get fixed. Dowse, dowse, dowse!

For several years I have been taking classes in reading the Tarot. I have a very competent teacher, but Tarot reading is very complicated, with many possibilities often open to interpretation. (It is also easier to read for someone else than to read for oneself.) So, when I'm doing a reading for myself, and I'm not sure of the message, I will whip out my trusty pendulum and dowse for the correct interpretation. After so many years of dowsing, I feel much more comfortable in my abilities to use the pendulum than in my ability to read the Tarot, so sometimes I just combine the two, and for me it works.

Well, I've given you a couple of suggestions. I'm sure that you can come up with more. Try them and see how they work. Practice **Yes** and **No** answers using Learning Chart A on page 32, and/or the *Maybe/Need more information* (as well as *Yes* and *No* answers) on Learning Chart B on page 41. Also, practice using the Percentage Chart which you will see on page 43.

The Percentage Chart

Now it's time for that Percentage Chart I wrote about earlier. The Percentage Chart is used when we want to get a more accurate answer than just a **Yes** or a **No**. This chart goes from 0 percent to 100 percent. You will notice that zero and 100 occupy almost the same spot. The way to know which percent is your correct answer, is by observing how the pendulum swings when you ask the question. The pendulum always swings back and forth starting at the zero spot, then moving backwards and forwards in a swinging motion, clockwise around the circle. The pendulum will stop moving clockwise when it is at the correct percentage, and will stay swinging in that same space, indicating what percent is the correct answer. Therefore, for 100 percent, the pendulum continues clockwise around the circle until it makes its way all the way around the circle and back up to the top.

To use the Percentage Chart, go through the preliminary steps for using the pendulum as usual, but when you ask the question, ask for what percent. The pendulum will swing in a clockwise direction and stop at the correct percent.

You can use this method to find to what percent or degree a certain supplement will be helpful. You can also ask as to what percent or degree you will be happy with the work of someone you need to hire to do a job for you (such as a painter, a landscaper, a plumber, a carpet layer, etc.)

Example: For Christmas 2005, I hand-dyed a dozen silk scarves as gifts for friends and relatives. As planned, the scarves all looked different. If you

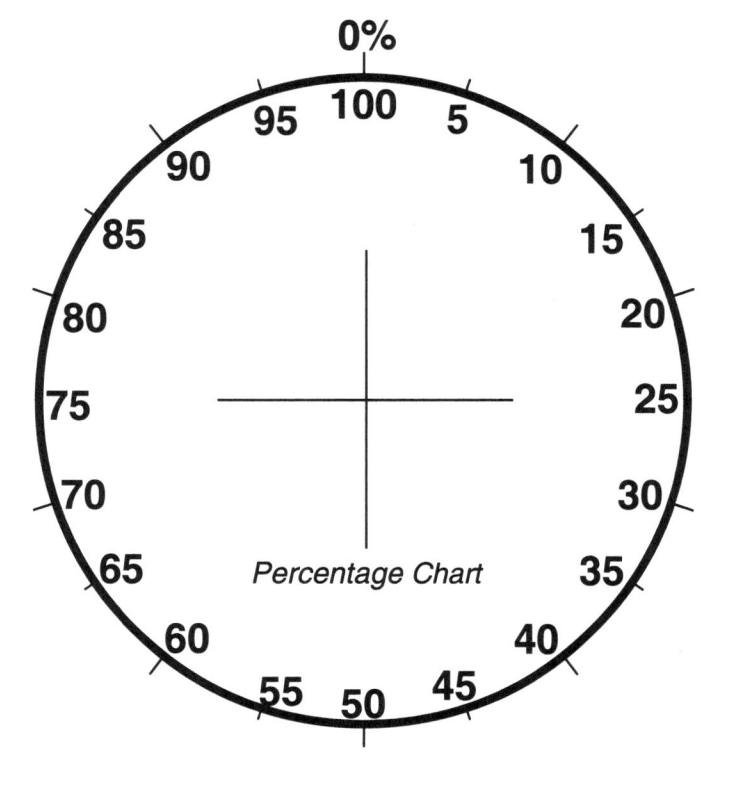

are like me, you could admire a dozen silk scarves, but only a few of these would work well in your wardrobe. Realizing this, I wanted each scarf I made to be the perfect one for the person who would receive it. So I dowsed each scarf. I wrote down the names of the people who were going to receive a scarf from me on a piece of paper, laid each scarf out on a table, and proceeded to dowse the individual scarves asking: "Would Mom like this scarf?" If she only liked one, then that one was hers, and was put to the side with her name on it. If she liked several, each was noted.

It helped to dowse each scarf and find out the percentage that a person would like each scarf. (Obviously a 100 percent "like rate" would beat out a 50 percent "like rate".) Then it was on to the next person, and the next, and the next, until all scarves and people were matched. This gift selection became a matching game through a process of elimination. As I was back in Missouri for Christmas, I got to see each person open their gift. It was such fun to see that each and every one of them liked the scarf they received; it was just the right color, just the right style for them, and matched what they liked to wear. The scarf I gave to my friend Theresa was just the right color for her skin tone, matches all of her wardrobe, and it is such a delight to see her wear it! Could I have been as accurate by just guessing who should get which scarf? I doubt it. Dowsing took all of the guesswork and stress out of it.

I showed you how to use the Percent Chart for buying and giving gifts and getting an accurate indication about how well a person may like a certain gift. Now you try asking some gift questions. Say you have a board game and you would like to know which relative to give this game to. Go down your list of names and ask: "To what percent would "name" (i.e., Uncle Bill, Aunt Millie, Cousin Joe, etc.) like this gift?'

When you find someone who would like the gift 100 percent, then you know you have a winner! Don't try giving the gift to someone who would only like the gift 50 percent or less because that would only be a waste. They wouldn't use the gift, and someone who would enjoy it has just lost out.

Another exercise would be to go down the list of movies in the newspaper and ask, "Will I enjoy watching this movie?" Dowse out all of the movies listed. Then dowse as to what percent you would enjoy watching them. When you get one that shows 90 to 100 percent, watch the movie. Then you can judge how accurate you were.

Remember—and this is important every time you dowse—when you are finished, remember to say "Thank you." This may seem silly to you, but you are given lots of divine help when you are dowsing, and you need to thank the spiritual helpers. You will always be insured that help will be there the next time you need it. (It would be there anyway, of course, but being thankful is always a nice thing to express.)

Energy work

I do a lot of energy work, and I like getting feedback on the work I do. Using the **Number Indicator Chart** (on page 46) will provide me with the information I need. For instance, many people ask me to cut the negative energy cords that are attached to their body.

With the help of Archangel Michael, I have established a way to successfully cut these cords—either with the person in front of me, or by long distance. After such a process, I then use the pendulum and the Number Indicator Chart to find out if all the negative energy cords have been cut, and just how many have been cut.

I also work with a group of friends in a *Circle*—along with our spirit guides, many angels, and several archangels—to help stranded souls cross over to the other side. After we have completed our work, I will check to see if all the souls we were trying to help have crossed over, and to see just how many crossed at

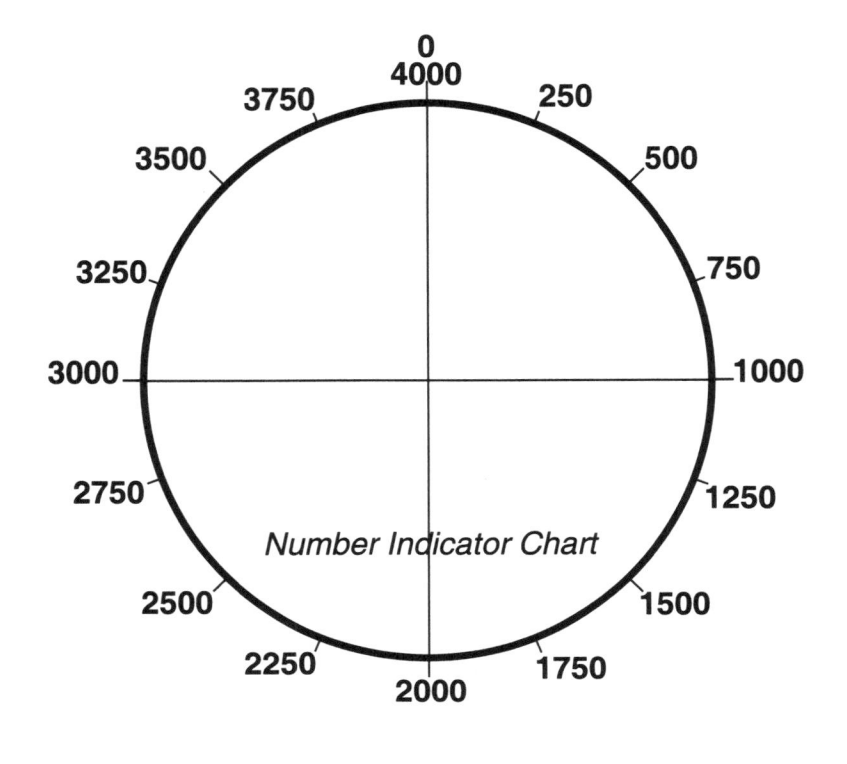

Number Indicator Chart

that time. I use the Number Indicator Chart to check this information. Sometimes, when doing this type of spiritual work, I do not have my chart in front of me. Then I will create a chart in "thin air". I will project a Number Indicator Chart in front of me, and point to different areas in that temporary chart, giving each point a numeric value: i.e., if the top of the circle is 0, a point at the right angle (90 degrees) may be 1000, the bottom of the circle will then be 2000, and to the left (90 degrees) will be 3000, with the top of the circle becoming 4000—if the pendulum makes the full circle.

Sometimes the numbers on a chart do not go high enough, so I will start over, giving each angular point of my temporary **Air Chart** a higher numeric value. This is **advanced dowsing,** so don't try this until you are very confident with all forms of dowsing, and you are able to visualize a chart in front of you. "Necessity is the Mother of Invention", and several years ago when I needed to dowse some information, and I did not have any of my usual charts with me, I created the **Flexible Chart.** It worked, and I have been using them ever since. The Flexible Chart has one distinct advantage: I can easily change the numbers on it if they do not go high enough, or represent the information I need. To help you make this giant leap in chart creativity, you will find a sample Flexible Chart on page 48.

At some point in your dowsing career, you will realize that the number charts I have created do not meet your needs, as the numbers do not go high enough. You may not yet be ready to make the leap into hyperspace, where you can confidently create your own Air Charts as I have just described. The Flexible Chart on page 48 is an interim tool, and you will most likely soon be using it with great confidence. In this chart, the numbers listed are only suggestions. You can use the numbers listed on the chart, or you can change them to fit your immediate needs.

Say you are seeking information regarding the purchase of a home, and you would like to know what price you should offer on the home you have just looked at. You want your offer accepted, but you don't want the offer to be too high either. Obviously, unless you are purchasing a home in a Third World country, the Number Chart which only goes to 4,000 will not be sufficient. Thus you need the flexibility of being able to change the numbers on the chart you are going to use.

If you are considering purchasing a double-wide mobile home, for instance, your number sequence may start at $0 (at the top of the chart), rise to $20,000 (at the right angle), to $40,000 (at the bottom), to $60,000 (at the left angle, to $80,000 (again at the top).

Tip: *Notice how the numbers suddenly became dollars. Yes, you can do that!*

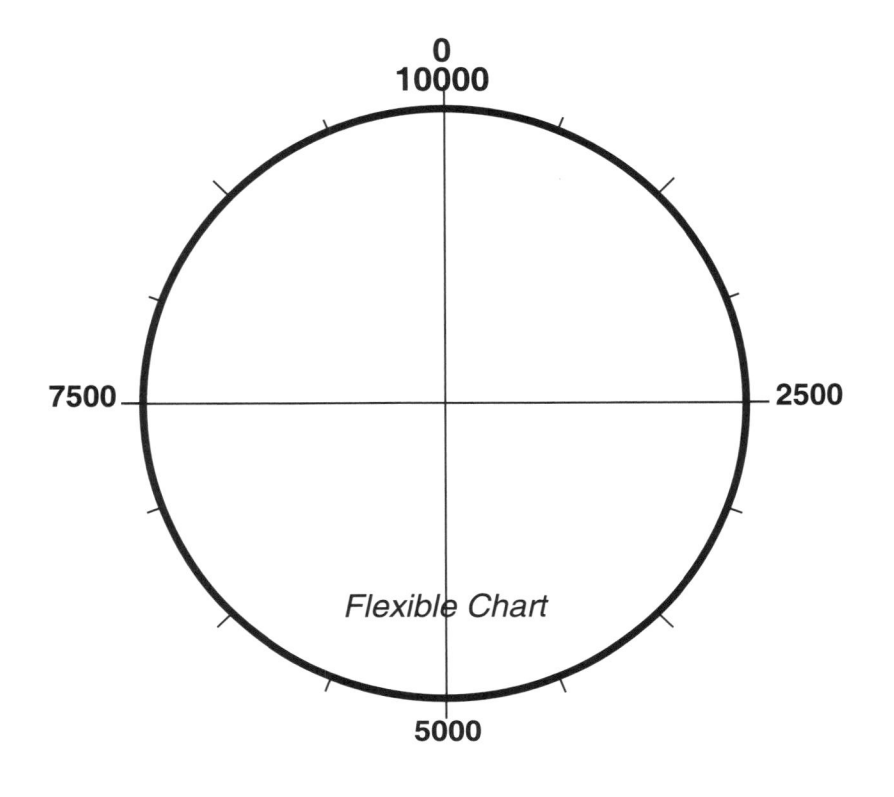

Flexible Chart

If you are looking to purchase a starter home in many parts of the United States, your number sequence may be from $0 to $50,000 to $100,000 to $150,000 to $200,000. But in other places in the United States, where homes go for much higher prices, you will have to be flexible in choosing the numbers to place on your chart. Your number sequence may have to be more like: $0 (at the top of the chart) to $150,000 to $300,000 to $450,000 to $600,000. The price all depends on the market and the normal price range of homes you are considering to buy.

When you first start using this chart you may want to lightly pencil in the numbers, but as you become familiar with using the chart, you will probably just state the number you wish to use, and touch that point on the chart (going around in sequence with appropriately spaced higher numbers). Always start with Zero at the top, move around the circle in a clockwise direction, and end with the highest number, once again at the top of your chart.

The pendulum will make an arc as it swings, starting at the top, traveling around the circle, until it comes to an appropriate number. Then the swing will remain in that spot. Often the swing will stop advancing between your anchor numbers, and you may not totally be sure of the correct number—especially when you are dealing with larger numbers.

These are the times when I will ask, "Is the number 460,000?", checking for a **Yes** or a **No** response. If I get a **Yes** response from the pendulum, I will know that this is the correct number. If I get a **No** response from the pendulum, I try again, perhaps asking, "Is the number 470,000?", once again checking for a **Yes** or **No** response. When the pendulum indicates **Yes**, then I have my answer.

As with all of the other charts, you will find this one quite useful, just as soon as you allow yourself the freedom to think outside the number box, so to speak. For me, the pendulum works best with questions leading to **Yes** and **No** answers, and questions leading to an answer in percentages or in numbers.

The next chart (on page 51), shows *negative* and *positive* responses. With this chart we will mainly use the top part of the circle, as this is where we will find the indicator number for most people. On the right side of the circle are positive numbers. On the left side are the negative numbers. At the very top is the 0 which is the *neutral* point. (Note that the *Ready for question* indication is still in the same spot as on the other charts you have worked with. It is indicated by a "?" at the +10 position.)

To practice using this chart, ask *"May I, Can I, Should I use this chart to obtain information about (name)?"* (The name you choose may be someone you know, politicians running for election, people I am interviewing for a job, etc…) If you receive a **Yes**, you can then state: *Ready for question,* and the pendulum will swing to the "?" mark. You will then state, "I want to check the character of (name). Please show me the position on this chart for this person." The pendulum will swing from the center pivotal point. Watch that point to be able to tell if the pendulum is swinging onto the positive side of the chart, or onto the negative side.

The Negative/Positive Chart is mainly used when checking the character of a person, but it can do much more. It can be used to check the energy and emotional state of a person. For instance, the chart can let you know if the person is negative, unhappy, depressed, or if the person is positive and happy in temperament.

There are times when it can be very helpful to know the character of people you are dealing with on a day-to-day basis. You may want to check out the possible new employee before you hire them, the people who want to rent from you, your new neighbor, your future son-in-law, someone you are dating, etc.

This chart is easily understood: positive or "+" is good, and negative or "-" is bad. On the plus side, the higher the number the "better" a person is. On this side of the chart you go from 0 or neutral to +5, a nice, honest person, all the way up to +50, a very desirable slot. The higher number a person is identified as having, the more other people want to be around them. They are happy, good natured, honest, and have very desirable characteristics. Plus 50 is about as good as it gets! We find very few people in this category; we might even categorize this person as "a saint". When someone reaches +50 they have reached Christ Consciousness, and live their life accordingly.

On the negative side, you will find people that are of a "lower" character. I'll give a little explanation of what that means. When someone is identified a -5, we often find the person to be dishonest; -10 is a minor thief; -15 is a major thief; -20 a serious criminal; -25 is dangerous. Minus 30 is a "murderer" (whether of hopes, dreams or actual people); -40, a mass murderer; -50 is a sociopath, a mass murderer, or serial killer—a person with no conscience; this is as bad as it gets. But as I stated earlier, the negative side can also reveal a person's current energy pattern, emotional state, and temperament. Minus 5 is unhappy, and the scale goes up in degrees until you get to -20 for an extremely unhappy, depressed being.

So the Negative/Positive Chart will give you a reading on a person's overall character. They may be higher in some positive traits than they are in others. For example, a person may have an overall character reading of +15, but you would

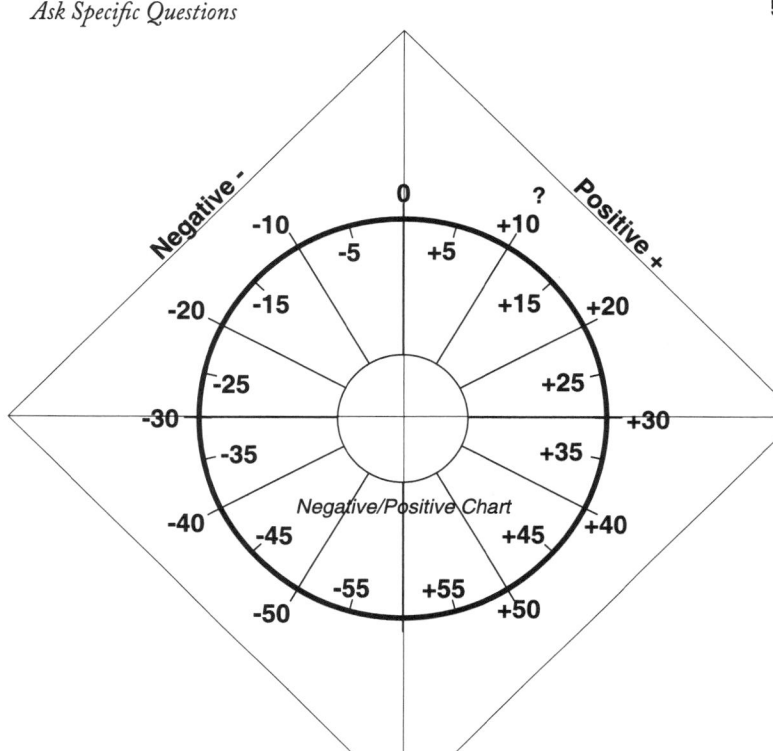

Negative/Positive Chart

like more information. They may rank +10 in regards to happiness, +20 in regards to spirituality, +15 in honesty. Other positive traits might be somewhere in between, and they may even have a few traits on the slightly negative side; but overall (as an average), they dowse out to a +15. This observation will let you know that they, overall, are a good person.

The same thing is true on the negative side, and here it can get even more convoluted. You may be dealing with someone who actually is a very good person, but who is temporarily (or often) so depressed that their personality shows up on the negative side. Depression is a very negative state of being, and can bring a person way down, real fast. So, to find out if the negative reading you get on a person is the result of depression or whether it indicates someone with a criminal nature, you can dowse out the information using one of the other charts. Use the charts you are familiar with to dowse a **Yes** or **No** answer. Don't forget, you can use the Percentage Chart for a percentage answer.

Another factor resulting in a reading on the negative side of this chart can be the result of drug use. In this instance both legal and illegal drugs can be the cause of the negative reading. Drugs can change a person's health, emotions, decision-making abilities, and many other factors, and can sometimes have a lasting effect on the personality. This effect can, in turn, affect someone's overall character. It is fair to say that, as a general rule, drugs affect a person in a more negative way than in a positive way.

Tip: *Try this chart out on yourself, then see your own numbers change as you grow spiritually and in other ways as you work with the information in this book. Try this chart out with some of our popular athletes, movie stars, world leaders, and local and national politicians; you may be amazed at what you find. This chart has many interesting possibilities. You may also be amazed when you dowse for yourself and see how your numbers change as a result of your personal growth!*

Family Line—No chart needed

I was a teenager when I first saw this method of dowsing, using a needle and thread with the needle stuck into the eraser part of a sharpened pencil. I didn't understand that what the grown-ups were doing was dowsing, and I doubt that any of them did either. We were all engrossed in what seemed to be a very interesting parlor game. One person was holding the pendulum (pencil on a string) over another person's left wrist, keeping track of the swing of the pendulum. I was so fascinated; this method could indicate the number and gender of the children I was going to have!

Everyone, of course, was interested and wanted to have it done on them. At that young age, I thought of it more as a game; now I realize that the information was correct, but the atmosphere in which it was done made light of the fact that accurate information was being given. One of the couples had 11 children, and for both husband and wife, each child was recorded—in the correct order, with the correct gender. My mother tried the test and not only were her four children indicated, but also the two spontaneous miscarriages.

Over and over again the same testing was done on dozens of people. The pendulum was accurate. Now, there were quite a number of us young people who had this testing done, and for us, children were part of our far distant future. So who's to say if what I saw that day was accurate in regards to that projection, but we certainly were fascinated. This was my first introduction to dowsing, though I didn't know it at the time.

Since I've become educated in the field of dowsing, I have often been asked to dowse for someone's Family Line. You do not need a chart for this particular technique; the person's left wrist becomes the chart. I do not use a pencil on a string; this gives the whole process the feel of a parlor game. (Dowsing doesn't need that; we already have enough skeptics to deal with.) I use my pendulum, holding it an inch or two over the other person's left wrist and ask, "What children will this person have?" If a girl, the pendulum will swing up and down, from hand to elbow. A boy will cause the pendulum to swing across the wrist.

In between each child there will be a break, indicated by the pendulum swinging in a small clockwise circle. There are usually only a couple of circular swings before the next indication. If there are quite a number of circular swings between children, it may mean that there will be many years between one birth and another. When all children have been indicated, the pendulum will stop swinging. All abortions and spontaneous miscarriages will be shown. Even pregnancies that lasted only a few weeks will be indicated. Sometimes the pregnancies were so short that the mother was not even completely sure that she was pregnant. If a person will have no children in this lifetime, the pendulum will do one of two things: it will not move at all, or it will make small clockwise circles and then stop.

One must use discretion when testing husbands and wives or engaged couples, because sometimes they do not get the same results. The reasons for this should be obvious! Many people may wonder how adoptions show up on this type of testing, and I have found that adoptions are not indicated. The child is truly theirs in bonding and in the context of legal forms, but he or she is not born of their flesh.

This gives rise to the question of in vitro fertilization, sperm banks, and other forms of medically induced pregnancies. Just how will these show up in this form of testing? I'm really not too sure. My gut feeling is that if your sperm created a child, it will show; and if your egg created a child, it will show. I just haven't had the opportunity to dowse in this type of a situation, so I just don't know what result I would get.

I can tell you that when I have done this type of dowsing, the results have been very accurate. I cannot tell you how often I've dowsed for someone I know, and instead of the pendulum swinging to indicate the one child they have, it will indicate two; or instead of 4, there will be six. The person will have had one or more spontaneous miscarriages that I did not know about, but they knew. This proves to them just how accurate this testing is.

I always go into this type of dowsing (and any other for that matter) with a totally open mind and with no preconceived notions. We must do this if we are to get truly accurate answers.

Dowsing for this type of information has caused me to give much thought to how much of our future is pre-destined and how much is free will. After mulling this over, I have come to the conclusion that when we come to this earth to live this life, we have already decided a number of important things that we want to accomplish and to experience. But we will have many choices in the manner in which these experiences are carried out and completed.

Being the mother of four children, I can say that having children is one of the most important things that we do in life; therefore, I believe that the number of children we will be conceiving is already imprinted in our future. With that being said, I believe that the type of dowsing just described can be accurately tested on a person, no matter what age they are. If you decide to test Family Line dowsing, try it on yourself first; and then when you do this for other people, do it with seriousness and respect.

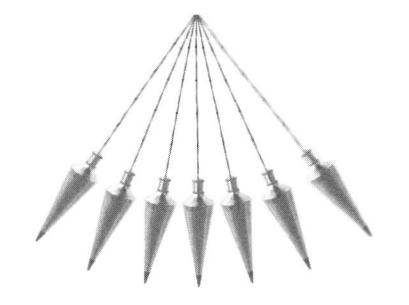

Chapter 5

Muscle Testing and Using the Body as a Pendulum

You may well wonder why I'm discussing muscle testing in a book about using the pendulum. Well, the body is the greatest pendulum of them all. After muscle testing using the arm and finger methods, I evolved the **Body-Pendulum Method** for self-testing, as well as one for client testing. These Body-Pendulum Methods are the ultimate in pendulum usage.

For the record, I am a Master Herbalist, Iridologist, Reflexologist, and a Reiki Master. Therefore, it became a very natural thing for me to use my skills working with energy to muscle test people regarding the use of nutritional supplements. I have used a variety of Muscle Testing techniques to discover which combination of herbs, which brands, and exactly how many pills an individual might need to take per day, bearing in mind what other supplements they may be taking. It did not take me long to become proficient at the usual methods of muscle testing.

It also did not take me very long to discover that I did not need to have the person in front of me holding the bottle of herbs in order to test them. I could hold the bottle while the person asking for my help could be thousands of miles away. These tests could be carried out with accurate results. Since this probably sounds like Greek to you, I will describe the whole learning curve that I experienced, so that you will be able to learn from my experience, and test these various methods for yourself if you wish.

The first thing I learned to do was to muscle test someone using their arm and my fingers in a resistance mode type of testing. It is established criteria that the stronger the resistance is when testing a person for a supplement, the more the person needs this particular supplement—because it will make them stronger. I first learned to muscle-test the **arm/finger pressure method,** then I learned to use the **thumb and forefinger method.** There is a time and place when each technique is preferable.

Next, I discovered that a person can test themselves by becoming a pendulum. Since this is a book about pendulum use after all, this is why I have included the technique in the book. I have learned that we are (our bodies are), in fact, the greatest pendulum of them all.

Anyway, after working with muscle testing people in person for some time, I realized that I did not have to have the person in front of me in order to carry out successful muscle testing. They could be thousands of miles away, and I could still test them accurately for the correct amount of supplements they needed. All I needed to know was the person's name, a little bit about them and their condition. And I needed to know the quality and suggested usage of the product being tested. (This is where being a Master Herbalist has helped a great deal.) The more information you have when you muscle test, the more accurate you can be. Of course, what we all want to do is to take any guesswork out of the equation; that's why we are dowsing. So read on, and I will explain in detail the process that I went through so that you can learn the techniques as well.

In muscle testing someone, the first thing you must tell the person is to make their mind blank; ask them to let go of any critical thoughts or judgments. (It will be hard to accurately muscle test them if they are thinking: "What should I make for dinner tonight?" "How much will this cost?" "I don't like taking pills!" "I don't want to be in pain one minute longer!" "What would so and so say?", etc.) Tell them to make their mind as blank as possible. You must also take your opinions out of the process. Thinking things like, "Wow, I could make a lot of money selling all these supplements!" will not produce accurate results. You must only have the welfare of the other person in your heart, or you will not be accurate in your testing. This means that you, too, should be non-judgmental. (We don't want to be picking up any negative karma when doing this work, so we must always work in the *light*, and for the greater good of all concerned.)

Muscle Testing

When I am muscle testing a person for the use of supplements (or anything else for that matter), I first make sure that they are electrically in balance. (Some people are not in balance electrically, and for the sake of accuracy, you must know this.) If the person is wearing a hat, have them remove it. Often a man will be wearing a billed hat and this bill gets in the way of me checking to see if they are electrically in balance.

To check that someone is electrically in balance, have the person stand in front of you, you facing them; however, you do not want them standing directly opposite you. Have them extend their right arm, and since you are facing them, you will be shifted a little to the left of their body. However, if they are using their left arm, have them extend their left arm, and since you are facing them, you will be shifted a little to the right of their body. You can use either their right arm or their left arm to muscle test. If someone has a weak arm or shoulder, do not use that one, use the strong arm and shoulder instead.

If the person is extending their right arm, use the first two fingers of either your right or left hand on their right wrist to do the testing. If they are extending their left arm, use the first two fingers of either hand on their left wrist to do the testing. You may or may not wish to place your other hand on their other shoulder when you get to testing the supplements. I have found no difference in accuracy if there is or is not a continuous **energy loop** between the two people.

Tip: *When doing this test, it is very important that you use a light touch. A light touch is even more accurate than a strong, forceful one. A strong, forceful test will wear them out, and you may not be able to carry out all the testing that is necessary. Also, it is important that the steps of the test are carried out all in one fluid motion. The person being tested needs to be told just enough so that they will understand the testing that is being done, and not so much that you lose them in the details.*

Now the testing can begin. You want the person to have a strong arm, not a weak arm when doing this test, so tell them so. First, standing in position, ask the person to extend their arm (the one you have decided to use for the muscle testing process). Use two fingers of one hand to press down on their wrist while saying "resist." Their arm should stay strong.

On the second test do the same thing. Ask the person to extend their arm. Now, using two fingers of one hand to press down on their wrist as before, simultaneously use the first two fingers of your other hand to touch their third eye point while saying "resist." You will find that this second time, the person's arm will swing down effortlessly. They will be amazed. This happens because their electrical circuit has just been broken.

Usually at this point, the person you are muscle testing will always want to know what just happened, or demand that you do it again. **Do not repeat a second time** just to satisfy their curiosity, as they will often try to sabotage you. Explain to them, as I told you, that their electrical circuit has just been broken, and that their response is just the way it should be. Now they are in balance for accurate testing.

If the "in balance" arm testing did not work properly, you may not have done things correctly. That can easily happen if you do not understand the directions I've given you above, or you have not had someone show you the correct way to carry out the test. Or, you may simply need more practice for things to flow smoothly.

The technique is actually very easy, but explaining it in writing is challenging. If this is a little confusing, just try again. Chances are it will work perfectly the second time. If it does not, and the person's arm does not swing down the second time, they may very well be out of balance.

If so, it will be necessary for the person to balance their electrical circuits. This is easily done with a series of cross-arm movements. The simplest way for a person to attain electrical balance is for them to first swing their right arm across their body to the left, and then their left arm across their body to the right. They should continue to do this exercise about a dozen times. (There are other ways to get a body electrically balanced, but this is the easiest one to explain.)

Tip: *Sometimes when carrying out the electrical balance check, the person's arm will not swing down because they are deliberately forcing it rigid. This will most often happen when a woman is testing a man. Men will take this "macho" stance, and will not allow any woman the "control" of getting a weak arm test. I can usually spot this tactic quite easily.*

Once you have determined that a person is electrically in balance, then you can accurately test them for supplements. As I mentioned before, strong resistance means that a person will need the supplement being tested; it will make them strong. Weak resistance means a person does not need that supplement; it will not help them.

Here is how to test someone's resistance to a supplement, using the arm technique described above: Have them hold the supplement in its container, in the hand/arm not being used for the testing, at the solar plexus (chest area) level. (Yes, you can accurately test through the container; it is not necessary to take the pills out of the container and hold one in your hand. I would not want to have the entire contents contaminated by someone accidentally putting the pill back in the container after testing because they didn't want to waste one.)

Then say, "Testing for product. Does (person's name) need this product?" Test using the **strong arm test**. If their arm stays strong, the supplement will be good for them. Repeat the process saying, "Does (person's name) need to take this product once a day?" Repeat asking twice a day, three times a day, etc., until their arm goes down. The last strong response is the correct one.

Now repeat the process, asking if the person needs to take one pill three times a day, two pills three times a day, etc., until their arm goes down. The last strong response is the correct one. (You can see why a person must use a light touch in doing this testing. If you use too much force, you will soon wear the person out, especially if they are old or weak to start with.)

Occasionally, when testing a supplement, the person's arm will not only hold strong, but will actually go up. When this happens, the person is really in need of the supplement. I've had people comment that they are already taking a supplement we are testing. When I ask how many capsules they are taking per day, they will often respond "One." Well, they are on the right track, but they are taking so few the supply cannot keep up with the demands of their body.

This happens often with arthritic problems. Say the person has had arthritis for 20 years. Their body is in lots of pain, and they think one herbal capsule for arthritis is enough. Get real! We're talking herbal supplements here, not strong pharmaceuticals! Individuals considering adding supplements to their diet usually need multiple capsules daily. Muscle testing is one way of showing them what their body does, indeed, need.

In addition to using the strong arm test, a person can also be tested by using the **thumb and forefinger resistance test,** a very accurate testing method. And, while it can be done, I do not recommend someone self-test in this manner. I have not found it to be as accurate for self-testing as the **Body-Pendulum Method** I will describe. However, before we go into that method,

I will explain the **thumb and forefinger resistance test**.

For the thumb and forefinger resistance test, you can test either the person's right hand or their left. Have the person form a circle with their thumb and forefinger. Hold their thumb with your right thumb above and your forefinger under their thumb. Hold their forefinger with your left thumb above and forefinger under (vise versa if testing using their left hand). Then say "resist" as you try to pull their thumb and forefinger apart. The person's thumb and forefinger should break apart.

This will give you a base level as to how strong their resistance is. I have tested a few men whose grip has been so strong that I have not been able to pull it apart. It is then necessary for me to use the thumb and middle finger. Once or twice I have had a person whose grip has been so powerful that I have had to use their thumb and ring finger.

Once you have established the individual's level of resistance you will be able to start muscle testing. Have them hold the supplement in the opposite hand at their solar plexus (as described previously in the general muscle-testing section); ask the same questions. Some people test better with their thumb and forefinger than they do using the arm testing method. This is especially true of the "macho" men I often deal with.

Each of us finds that a certain percentage of people are impossible to muscle test. Their belief system will block your ability to do the testing. They may simply not believe that it is possible to test anything in this manner, or they may not believe that you, of all people, could know how to do this. They may never even have heard of this technique! These people may or may not be the same ones who have a hard time believing that other forms of dowsing or pendulum usage can work. They may be very religious people who believe in God or a Creator, or they may be atheists who do not believe in a higher power at all. If they consider themselves to be religious people, it is difficult for me to understand why they don't believe that our Creator could have created a form of energy without creating an equally necessary ability to access the information in order to work with that energy. If they believe that each of us is created in the Creator's image, why shouldn't you be the one who would have such knowledge and such skill?

Such people will often remark that if it were possible this type of energy work was important/real, that then doctors would know the techniques and would use them in their work. Would that this were so! This type of testing could save us all so much pain and uncertainty (not to mention, money); some patients might be able to discontinue their treatments or pharmaceuticals (perhaps remove the necessity of taking some drugs in the first place—drugs that may be harmful or that don't help us), by instead zeroing in on the one drug or treatment that would be helpful.

But just so you know, a great many chiropractors and other alternative health professionals use muscle testing in their practice (often using the word ***Kineseology*** to describe the technique). Often they will be testing you when you are not even aware of it. Many chiropractors and Master Herbalists find it a most reliable means of helping their clients.

It is possible to test children if their parents allow it and they are old enough to understand—and can hold a strong arm. One of the first children I muscle tested was a young boy with asthma who had been on asthma medication for years. His mother was concerned about the negative side effects of the medication, and wanted to try an alternative method of treatment.

Like many people she was skeptical; after all, if herbs worked why didn't doctors use them? (If I only had a dollar for every time I've been asked this question!) Well, I was able to test the young man who was at that time 10 or 12 years old. We found out that he needed to take two supplements, both excellent for people with asthma. He started on these immediately, and within a month he just stopped taking his medicine; he no longer needed his inhaler. He also no longer experienced the emotional roller-coaster that his medication had produced.

He and his parents went on a 150-mile trip into the Alaska bush, and he didn't take his drugs along. When his mother found out she started to panic, but decided it would be best to just calm down. If her son needed his asthma medication, they would deal with it when the time arose. Her son just continued to take the two herbal supplements and, fortunately for them, all went well. The family kept in touch with me for several years, and the last I heard from them, the son never needed the asthma medication after that first month while the supplements were phased in.

I could share hundreds of these stories. And, yes, each of us is capable of reading the books and using the information on product labels to decide which vitamins, minerals, and supplements would be good for us to take for whatever the condition. By muscle testing we are just so much more accurate. Even when I do an Iridology reading (looking in a person's eye to see which health conditions and physical problems are represented in the iris), and I use the MRM machine (Muscle Response Monitor) to test the 60 body systems to find out the weakest system in order to determine which herbal supplements are most needed to restore their body to health, I will still muscle test the person. The reason is that there may be three supplements that would benefit the patient almost to the same extent. I need to know which of the three is the best for the individual, how often they need to take it, and the quantity their body needs.

The interesting thing about herbal supplements is that they, unlike pharmaceuticals which have unwanted side effects, have **_side benefits_**. When we muscle test, we are testing for the side benefits, right along with the main purpose for taking the particular supplement.

Surrogate muscle testing

There is also something known as **surrogate muscle testing**. This is a technique I use when a person is too weak or too young for me to muscle test reliably. Mothers make wonderful surrogate testers. The child being tested will hold the supplement, and the mother will hold or touch the child. Then I will use the mother's free arm to strong arm or thumb and forefinger resistance test. I have found this to be a very accurate and reliable method of testing. If a person has any question about accuracy, they can cross check by using the pendulum, or by employing the following method.

Body-Pendulum Method

After using the several methods of testing supplements described previously, I learned that people could test themselves with the Body-Pendulum Method. In this method, I prefer testing someone without their shoes on; but this is not necessary if they have shoes that allow them to maintain their balance, i.e., no high heels.

First I test to see if they are electrically in balance. This is done by having them say "Yes": they should tilt forward without getting up on their toes. I have them say "No": they should tilt backwards. If the results are opposite, the individual is not electrically in balance; they will then need to perform the crossed arm procedure explained earlier. When in balance, proceed. Have the individual hold the supplement being tested to their solar plexus, and repeat the question: "Do I need this supplement?" or "Is this supplement good for me?"

I always stand to the side of the person as they carry out this step, so that I can see their "sway". Sometimes it is very slight, and they may not even be sure that they are moving; but from the side I will be able to detect it. Other times the sway may be so strong that they almost fall over; then I am close enough to catch them. This has happened a lot. Indeed, it happened to me the first time I tested using this method. I was testing to see if I should be using cayenne. Luckily I was standing next to the bed, because the pull was so strong that I fell down on top of it during the testing process! (The reason I was considering the cayenne was that I had been having migraines for several years; when I tested the cayenne, my need for it was so strong I was completely pulled over by it.)

Occasionally, when doing this type of testing, a person will sway in circles. That means that they don't know the answer. Sometimes this occurs when they don't know what the particular supplement is for, or if they simply do not have enough information. When this occurs, it is best if someone else will muscle test for them. I have found that when this happens to me, if I just take one of the supplements orally, I will then be able to correctly test the supplement with the Body-Pendulum Method because my body now understands the quality and purpose of that supplement.

Since I have used the Body-Pendulum Method for so many years, I no longer have to ask any questions when I am testing myself. My body knows what is going on. I just have to hold the supplement in my hand by my solar plexus, and I will automatically start to sway forward or backward. I really like to demonstrate this method. It's easy to show people and for them learn to use it for themselves within just a few minutes. It is the fastest of all methods.

I have also learned that I can use the Body-Pendulum Method to test on behalf of other people, sometimes with them being in the room, sometimes on the telephone, and sometimes with them thousands of miles away. It is awesome! If you want to test this method yourself, just make sure that there is no doubt that you are testing for another person by clearly stating that you are testing for (person's name) and not yourself.

I first learned I could do long distance body-pendulum testing when faced with a situation in which it was necessary. My dad had been in the hospital in Missouri and almost died because of a blood clot. He was in very serious condition and when he came home from the hospital after a ten-day stay, he was so weak that he could only walk a few steps. The family had to move his bed into the living room. Also, one of his legs was so swollen that the skin tore in numerous places. According to my mother, this leg was twice as big as the other one.

I was in Alaska at the time and could not go back to Missouri; my then husband was back in Missouri because his father was in the hospital and was dying. I needed to stay in Fairbanks with our children, my business and all the other things that required me to be there.

My ex-husband had taken my MRM machine (muscle response monitor) with him so that he would be able to do testing while he was in Missouri. The MRM machine is a system that tests 60 systems of our bodies and lets us know which is the weakest. One is then able to use the machine to test those supplements designed for the systems, finding out which of them a person needs most. (This is a great machine for people who want to see this type of information in print.)

Anyway, after my dad came home from the hospital, he finally asked to start using herbs as he realized that modern drugs were only keeping him alive and not making him better. My ex-husband wanted to check with me about the results he got since he was not as proficient with the MRM machine as I was (after all I had been certified on it and had been using it for years).

I selected a variety of supplements I thought my dad might need from my shelf, and used my body to do the body-pendulum testing. (I stated that I would be testing these products for my dad.) As a result of the testing, I created a list: how many, how often, and why he needed them. Then my ex-husband and I compared notes. There was only one supplement he had listed that I did not. I immediately sent these supplements to my dad, and he started using them right away. Dad's doctor saw remarkable improvements in him almost immediately; the swelling went down in his leg and he was getting stronger. The doctor kept asking what dad was doing, and finally my mom confessed to the doctor that dad was taking herbal supplements. The doctor told him to keep doing whatever he was doing because the swelling in his leg would not have diminished as a result of the medications the doctors were prescribing.

My dad experienced a remarkable recovery and within six months he was back farming again. Not bad for a man who was 75 at the time! Mom and dad celebrated their 60th wedding anniversary last year with a huge party. As of this writing, dad is 86, works every day, and is still going strong.

When you start practicing the muscle testing methods I have explained to you, it would be best if you first practice with a friend who has similar beliefs to your own. Sometimes family members may think you are a bit odd if you try learning with them, and they can try to thwart your efforts. You and your friend should practice until you both feel confident before you start using these new skills with someone else.

I have taught hundreds of people how to muscle test themselves and to muscle test others. But the greatest thrill is when I show people how to body-pendulum test. People are in awe when they see that they can do this. It is very empowering. People feel they no longer have to be stuck in a circumstance, uncertain about what might be good or bad for them to take.

You see, now they can also test food (a much appreciated and wonderful thing for people who have food allergies), in addition to testing any medications they may have been prescribed. People are often greatly surprised to find the medications they are taking are not as good for them as they may have hoped, sometimes doing more harm than good. The ability to test the prescriptions (and supplements) they have been given provides individuals with the knowledge/insight they need to make informed decisions: "Would it be better to find a different drug, one that doesn't adversely affect me?" Or, "Would I be better off taking a natural supplement?"

Muscle tests and the body-pendulum test (as well as the use of the pendulum for testing)—all offer people a way to start living a healthier lifestyle, because they now have a way of ascertaining what is best for them. Also, since each individual's needs can change over time (indeed, sometimes daily due to a variety of factors: stress, lack of sleep, diet, excess work, fighting a virus, recovering from surgery, etc.), they can test to be sure they are taking the appropriate amount of vitamins, minerals, and other supplements at any given time.

You can use your body in the different muscle testing techniques, or you can use your pendulum to find out this same information. As you commence your journey of self-discovery, start by using your pendulum and the Percentage Chart. Have the bottle of herbs, prescription drug(s), food, etc., in front of you and ask, "May I, Can I, Should I dowse to find out if this (name item) is good for me (or, for whomever you may have been asked to dowse)? Ready for question."

When you get the indication that the pendulum is ready for you, ask if it (the item you are testing) is good for you. Ask if you should be taking it, will it help you, will it hurt you, how much to take, and how often, etc. Using the Percentage Chart, ask to what percent this (name item) will help you. The pendulum will then swing back and forth in a clockwise manner until it comes to the percentage this item will help you.

Kinesiology

Muscle testing is also known as **Kinesiology**. Kinesiology is a way of testing the physical body and of performing emotional release techniques. I took courses from Dr. Victor Frank to learn how to use kinesiology to release deep seated emotions. We will not explore this topic here as it is a very detailed and complicated subject that takes much time to learn. I will mention, though, some of the physical types of testing one can do with kinesiology. I don't expect to be able to explain the techniques here in sufficient detail for you to be able to perform them, but just enough for you to know what is possible.

First, one must have a good comprehension of the function of the various body parts and their location in the physical body, i.e., the liver is on the right side of the body behind the front lower rib cage; the appendix is at the bottom of the cecum located in from your right hip bone about two inches. In order to muscle test certain body parts, we must know where they are.

I test using the strong arm/weak arm technique. After asking permission to touch their body, I place my right hand on the body part in question and ask to test the liver, gall bladder, appendix, etc. If their arm responds very weakly by swinging down, they probably have a problem with that part of their body. If their arm stays rock solid strong, that part of the body is healthy.

This, in a nutshell, is how to use kinesiology. There is, of course, a lot more to it, but I just wanted you to know that such testing is possible, and is very accurate when preformed by someone who has had training and is an expert kinesiologist.

Warning about doubters

Now, here is a word of warning regarding demonstrating the use of the pendulum to others (indeed, all forms of dowsing and muscle testing)! If there is someone around you when you do this work who is extremely negative, or who casts great doubt about the purpose or potential outcome of what you are doing, or who is skeptical about how these techniques work, you will not get accurate answers.

Many years ago I was asked to give a demonstration regarding dowsing at the high school my children attended. It was for one of the science classes. The way I was approached, I thought they wanted to actually learn about dowsing, and to see some demonstrations.

As it turned out, the teacher wanted to debunk what I was doing, and so did many of the students. Because of this hostile atmosphere, my dowsing was not very accurate. Their energy of wanting to prove me wrong was stronger than my energy of being accurate because I was greatly outnumbered in the classroom.

This experience did teach me a great lesson, and one well learned. Do not teach, give demonstrations, or work with someone who does not believe that what you are doing is viable. The more people doubting, the greater their influence will be. Now I only work on or for people who believe the process can or will work, and who have faith in what can be done for them.

When dowsing a well, for instance, I have no problem when the person hiring me to dowse the well stays with me when I do this work. They wouldn't pay me to find water for them if they didn't want a well—indeed want one with good quality water, good flow rate, and at a depth they could afford to put in. Almost everyone I dowse water for is so amazed that they want a quick lesson in finding water. They want to give it a try themselves!

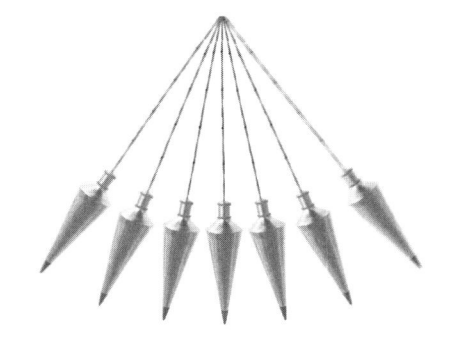

Chapter 6

My Start as a Dowser

When people find out that I'm a dowser, they always want more information because most have never met one before. (I'm not sure if we are supposed to look different or what?) So, hold on, here's the full story.

I was about 28 years old at the time, living in the country in Fairbanks, Alaska. My husband and I were thinking of selling our home but keeping the back six acres and drilling a well on it. We asked our friend, Charlie Lasater, to come over to dowse a well because he was the only dowser we knew.

By the time I came out of the house, Charlie had already located a well site, but I didn't know this. Charlie had a forked tree branch in his hand and he gave it to me, showed me how to hold it, and said, "Here, why don't you see if you can find water." I had no idea what I was doing, but I followed his instructions and started walking over the land. The next thing I knew, greatly to my surprise the twig went down—and went down with a surprising pull! I had just walked over the underground stream. I was told to look to my right and I would see the marker that they had just staked a few minutes ago. It was right next to where I had gotten the response. Charlie said, "You're a dowser." I sure didn't know much about anything to do with dowsing, but I could do it.

Asa, my husband, said, "Let me have that thing." He took the tree branch, held it just right and walked and walked all over the same spot. But there was no reaction. (Made him a little bit mad that I could do it and he couldn't.) Little did I know that that seemingly inconsequential act of dowsing would set in motion a learning curve, one that would take many years to unfold. Over the years I would learn more about dowsing than I could ever have imagined possible!

With hard work and practice, Asa has been able to learn how to dowse, but he had to be trained. For me it came naturally; I don't know exactly why. As the children were born and got older, they have all tried "holding the twig." My son Ace was also able to dowse naturally; my three girls could not. My dad can dowse, but most of my relatives cannot. And they are also always surprised when they see the results of our dowsing.

I do know that over the years I've been able to train many people how to dowse—some were naturals and others not. I don't know for sure why. I certainly had no belief one way or the other when I held that first tree branch. I do know that for many years I could not wear a watch and have it keep accurate time, so sometimes I wonder if magnetic energy may have something to do with it? It's quite possible that our connection with the Divine Creator could be a factor, and there is also the possibility that our auric energy is a factor. Any number of factors may cause a person to be a natural; but I also know that, without a doubt, people can be trained to be dowsers. They just need someone who can teach them the 4-Step Program; they need to believe that they can learn, and then practice so that they keep up the skill they were just taught. And to become consistently accurate, they need consistency in use.

There's been a lot of learning going on

You may be asking yourself, "How did this lady find out all of this information?" Honestly, a lot of the knowledge just came to me. Sometimes I just needed to know something and the information came; I tried it and it worked. But this was only after I had put in many years of slowly learning and increasing my skills. I really didn't start to make progress in dowsing until after I joined the Dowsers Society in Fairbanks, Alaska. This was a great group of people who were wonderful about sharing information and experiences. It was as though we were all learning together.

If you are interested in dowsing you may want to connect with an organization called the ***American Society of Dowsers.*** They hold yearly meetings and have a bookstore that contains a wealth of information. One book I bought there helped me learn so much: ***Letter to Robin—a Mini-Course in Pendulum Dowsing*** by Walt Woods. This book explained about programming your dowsing system. I learned that it was possible to dowse only for good, palatable water. (Why even find a stream of water if it is only going to supply undrinkable water after we drilled the well? Of course, you can put in a water treatment system to remove hardness and rust from your drinking water, but why go to that expense if you can dowse for the best quality water possible on a parcel of land?) This was an eye opener!

I next learned about an organization known as ***ORI***, or ***Ozark Research Institute***. They are located in Fayetteville, Arkansas, and their purpose is to increase awareness and learning regarding all forms of energy work. They hold seminars three times a year, and I was fortunate enough to be able to attend one of these seminars. The one I attended was a 5-day seminar.

Each day we had a different teacher. These teachers spent a full day sharing their knowledge and skills with a classroom full of different students each day. There I was, a babe in the woods, meeting teachers who had knowledge to share—knowledge beyond anything I could have imagined. Walt Woods was one of my teachers, and he spent a full day explaining dowsing. That man knows his stuff! Then I met Raymon Grace who talked about energy and hands-on healing. Again, another star! We even had lectures with group participation every evening.

After a week of this, my head was so full of new ideas and information that I was changed forever. At this seminar I made several lifelong friends. After I got back home to Fairbanks, I shared a lot of this knowledge with the Fairbanks Dowsers Society as well as with the bi-weekly Healing Circle I hosted in my home. My friends were just like me—we wanted to know more and more and more.

Then I put myself out on a limb. With the help of some other dedicated people, we were able to invite some of these expert teachers to Fairbanks, to have them conduct seminars with us. Over the following decade, Harold McCoy (the president of ORI), Raymon Grace (healer, lecturer and author), and Delores Cannon, (lecturer and author) stayed at my home and conducted seminars in Fairbanks. Not only was it an honor having them stay with my family and me, but we became friends. These three people shared more than just information; they shared themselves.

These and other wonderful, knowledgeable people guided my studies. I have also purchased and studied hundreds of books and reference materials on energy work, herbs, alternative healing and related topics; and taken the time to practice, practice and practice some more. All of this work helped form the professional I have become—indeed, the person I am today. Based on this background, I share my knowledge with you in writing this book.

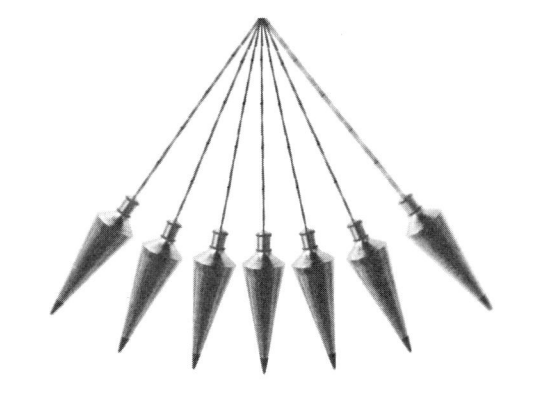

Chapter 7

Y-Rods & L-Rods: Dowsing for Water Veins

Over the years I have had numerous teachers and co-learners in all forms of dowsing and muscle testing. I have learned there is a lot more to these skills than just holding a forked tree branch and walking over property! My favorite **Y-Rod** (called a Y-Rod because it is shaped like the letter "Y") is made of plastic. Most dowsers will prefer a twig or tree branch as their Y-Rod; in fact, it is not uncommon to find dowsers who will argue about the type of twig or branch that should be used for dowsing.

There are dowsers who will not believe that you can dowse for water with anything but a peach tree twig. Well, there aren't any peach trees in Alaska, and there are water dowsers in Alaska, so how do they reconcile this? There are also people who will only dowse with a willow branch because they believe that is the only way you can find water. Wrong again! Willow trees don't grow everywhere, and dowsers still find water. My favorite Y-Rod is always available to use, I don't ever have to go out looking for one. In Alaska finding the right twig can be a problem in the deep of winter. You would have to go tromping in several feet of snow to get to the tree, only to find brittle branches to work with because all the sap has gone down. No, for me that little piece of plastic works just fine.

There is another problem with tree branches as Y-Rods, when you can find them: one side of the forked branch will be thicker than the other side. This causes warping or twisting when you find water and the branch goes down. I've even had some pulls so strong that the branch breaks or the bark pulls off, and that's hard on my delicate little hands. No, that little plastic Y-Rod is my favorite: it's just as accurate as any twig around. It's the **dowser** that makes the difference, not what the Y-Rod is made of!

I've also learned that there's quite a bit to know about dowsing if you want to be accurate and you want to find a good underground stream of water. When I first started I thought that finding water was just finding water. Then we dug our first well in Alaska. The water was rusty, foul tasting, foul smelling, and you would think that a dinosaur was still down in that pool of water. After this, I learned that you want water from a running stream; you do not want to dig a well where there is an indication of just a big round pool of water. We have a lot of bad wells in and around Fairbanks, Alaska; the water just isn't fit to drink.

That's when I learned that the dowser can program him- or herself to only find good tasting water—water that is free of rust, odor, and contaminants. I also learned that I could set other parameters when I dowsed for water. Before dowsing and after surrounding myself with protection and white light, I would state that I only wanted to find water that was less than 100 feet deep, 150 feet deep, 200 feet deep, or what ever was appropriate for that part of the country. When drilling for water in Missouri or other locations that have a requirement that the water to be drilled must be under a layer of clay or solid rock, I will state that this is the only stream of water I want to find. Therefore, part of the state drilling code becomes a temporary parameter I set for this one specific dowsing situation.

I usually also state the amount of flow rate that will be acceptable; in most cases I want a flow rate of at least 7 gallons of water per minute. And I state that I am looking for the best well water on the specific plot of ground, in a location close to where the house will be built, but far enough away from the septic system to meet requirements. I also state that the well to be found will be at a depth that is affordable to put in (this is where I state how many feet is an acceptable depth).

Tip: *If you are dowsing a well, make sure that you state that you are only looking for good, palatable water.*

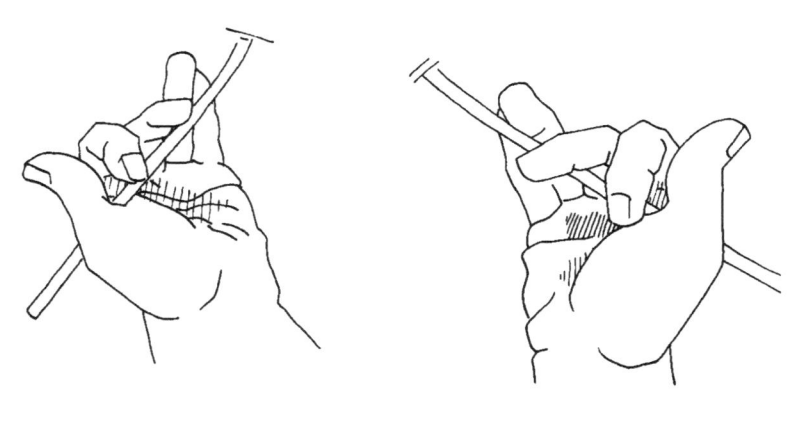

Wow, I had no idea that a person could state all of these requirements when I held my first Y-Rod those many years ago.

Have you ever wondered why that piece of plastic or that tree branch is called a Y-Rod? It's quite simple really. It's called a Y-Rod because that is the shape the branch or plastic rod is in when you hold it in your hands in the dowsing position.

For the Y-Rod to be able to work, you must hold the Y-Rod correctly in your hands. With elbows bent, hold the Y-Rod a little above waist high with your palms up, so that the thumbs are pointed to the outside. Grip the ends of the Y-Rod with about an inch of rod sticking out from the thumb. You will walk with the rod held parallel to the ground but with the tip of the rod at a slight upward tilt. As you walk slowly over the property, your only thoughts should be about finding water. You already are grounded, have the white light of protection around you, and you're in the "energy zone". You are mentally prepared to find water.

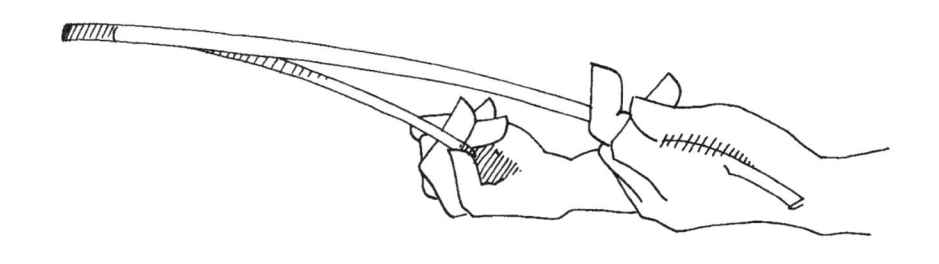

The first thing I do when walking onto a piece of property to find water is to ask where they plan to put the house, the driveway, and the septic system. I also need to know if these locations can be changed in case the only good underground stream and place to drill for it is right where one of these structures might be located. If the property is already built on, and everything is already in its place, then you have to work keeping these factors in mind (i.e. you need to be the required distance from any septic system, whether on your own property or that of your next door neighbor; and you don't want to drill so close to the house that any future additions (such as a garage) will put the well

head under it, or so close to it that pulling a well pump in the future becomes impossible. It is important to keep all of these factors in mind.

Then I will do what my old friend Charlie Lasater called "smelling for water". I will hold the Y-Rod in my hands, and slowly turn in a circle. I will feel a sense, a pull in a certain direction. That is the direction I always start walking. It is usually there I will find the best stream of water.

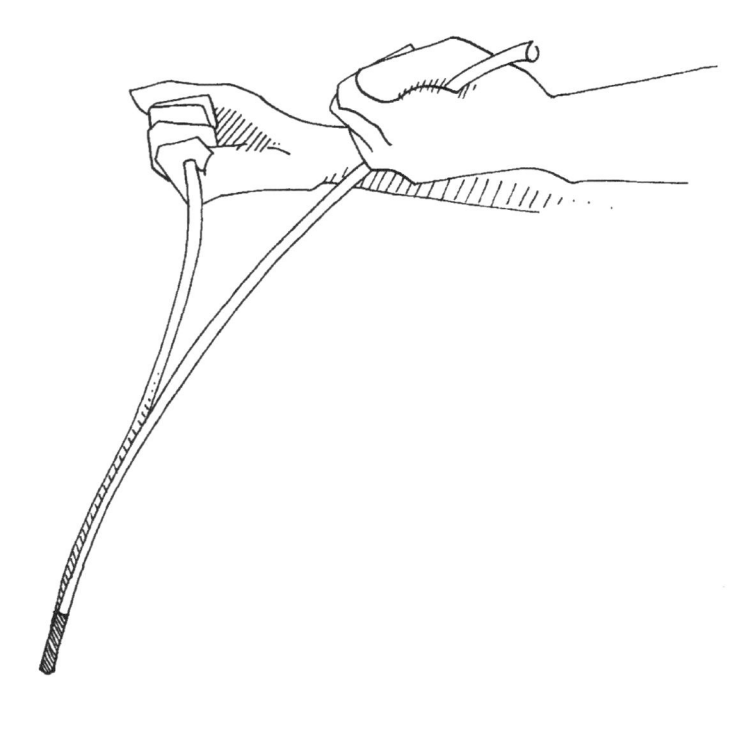

I now walk slowly over the property. I've "smelled the water" so I have an idea of which direction to walk. I hold my Y-Rod gripped tightly in my hands, with the point slightly pointed upward—about 45 degrees (see diagram on page 79). When I walk over the stream, the Y-Rod will swing down to the ground. The stronger the swing, the greater the amount of water to be found, or the shallower the depth.

When I find a stream, I will dowse to determine if this is the best stream of water for a well on the property. If I get an indication that there is a better location or stream on the property, I will keep searching until I find the very best one. After I find the best water on the property, I want to stake out the stream. I do this by going back and fourth over the territory for about twenty feet. I stake the stream in three or four places; wooden 12" surveyor stakes work well. This will identify the line in which the stream is actually flowing underground. Somewhere along that line is where they will drill for water. I keep in mind the lay of the land, the locations of the home, driveway, septic system, etc. Then I put in the master stake, identifying the place where the well-driller will drill.

Tip: *Make sure that you tie surveyor's tape on this master stake so that it does not become confused with the other stakes. Also, write on the stake the depth at which the water should be found.*

There is also a little dowsing tool known as the **L-Rod.** It also gets its name from its shape. The short part of the "L" is held in your hand, and the long part of the "L" sticks out and is able to swing freely. You can get a lot of information using this tool to dowse for water.

The L-Rod I like best is the **Sleeved L-Rod** (patent pending). This L-Rod is far from the bent metal coat hanger of the past. This rod has a sleeve on the short end, the end which you hold in your hand. The L-Rod can then swing freely without you touching it at all.

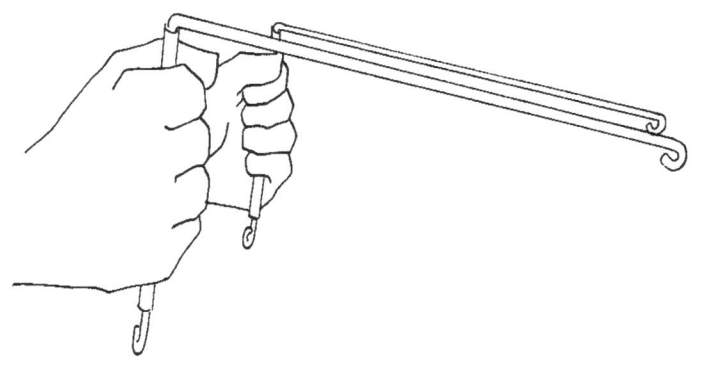

This helps achieve extremely accurate dowsing results. (Plus, skeptics find it easier to believe that you're not manipulating the rod when you can't touch it directly.) The other great factor that makes this L-Rod unique is that it has a large loop at the long end. The loop on the end of the tool can slip over a belt loop, making it possible to keep this instrument with you while your hands are then free to use another dowsing instrument.

I actually have 3 sets of L-Rods—small, medium, and large. The small rods are easy to carry and fit in my purse; they are only 6 inches long. The medium size is 9 to 10 inches long; the large size is 12 inches long but made of heavier gauge metal. I like the large L-Rod for dowsing wells because the heavier weight will keep the wind from moving them and giving false readings. I use the small and medium size ones for checking the layers of auras, and for other energy work.

You can use the L-Rods to determine how wide the stream of water is. Hold your L-Rods in hand and walk over the stream of water, crossing the stream to the other side. The rods will swing either both out or both in when you hit the first edge of the stream. Walk slowly and they will cross each other when you are in the center of the stream. Continue walking and the L-Rods will once again swing either out or in when you cross the other edge of the stream. With my boots I make a mark in the ground at each edge so that we can subsequently determine how wide the stream is (some are wide at 5 to 6 feet, and others very narrow at only a foot or less).

Tip: *The narrower the stream, the more accurate a well driller needs to be. If his rig is not sitting level when he drills, he can miss the stream because the drill stem will go down at an angle.*

After I find my best stream of water on a property and it is all staked out, then I want to know the direction the water is flowing in, the depth of the water, and the flow rate. All this can be determined using the L-Rod. Holding only one L-Rod in my right hand, I stand directly on the spot in which the Y-Rod went down (the drilling spot).

When I get a *Yes* answer, the rod will swing and point to my chest. When I get a *No* answer, the rod will swing parallel to my body. Therefore, when I ask if this is the best stream of water on the property for a well that meets all of the criteria mentioned above, I will get a **Yes** if the L-Rod points to my chest and a **No** if it points to the right or left side of my body. If **No**, I will keep looking. If **Yes**, I will ask how far down they will have to drill to reach water.

Here is an example: I start by asking if the well depth is 100 feet. I may get a slight swing inward. Next 120 feet, 140 feet, 160 feet and so on until the point of the rod is pointing directly to my chest. Say the L-Rod points directly at my chest at 200 feet, if I say 210 feet the L-Rod will swing a little beyond my chest, which indicates that 210 feet is too deep. If I say 250 feet and the L-Rod swings even further from the center of my chest, this lets me know that 250 feet is way too deep. So, now we have found our depth.

Next I'll ask about the direction of the flow of the water in the underground stream. The L-Rod will point in that direction. My next question is to find out how many gallons per minute to expect from this stream. I will ask if the flow rate of the water will be 5 gallons per minute, and the L-Rod should swing in slightly. I then ask 6 gallons per minute, 7 gallons per minute, etc., checking each time to see how the rod reacts. When the rod points directly at my chest I know that I have hit on the correct number of gallons per minute.

The bobber

There is another instrument called the bobber. It consists of a flexible rod or wire that is 2 to 3 feet long, with a wooden handle on the end that you hold. The other end is coiled with a weighted tip. It should be very flexible. I personally do not like using the bobber, but if you do, then by all means continue to use it. Bobbing up and down will give you a **Yes,** and a swing sideways gives you a **No.**

The problem I find with a bobber is that when one wants to find the depth of a well, it is quite time consuming and one needs to keep focused in order to get an accurate count. For instance, when asking the depth of a well, the bobber will bob once for each foot to the level of the water! For a 500 foot well you are going to be counting a long time—496, 497, 498, 499, 500. Get the picture? When the bobber finally stops, I hope you didn't miscount too many times. I personally have just not felt comfortable with a bobber, so I don't use one.

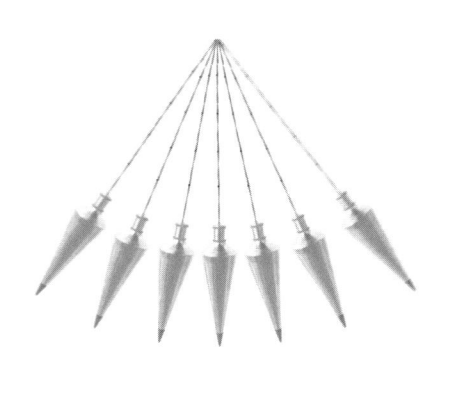

Chapter 8

Keeping a Log

I keep a spiral bound set of index cards for logging my well dowsing. They contain the date, name of person requesting services, phone numbers, location of property, and directions to property. I note the depth and gallons per minute that I projected. I ask that the person then contact me after the well is dug, so that they can let me know how the drilling went. I will make notes as to how deep the well went, how many gallons per minute they have, and what well drilling company they used. This will keep a record of how accurate I am. It also allows me to refer people to the better well drillers in the area once I have a number of references.

Tip: *Note that the well drillers will often punch in the well 10, 20, or more feet deeper than the depth at which they found water so that there will be a little reservoir for the water to collect in. This is a good thing, but the extra depth* *can make it look like you were off on your well projection. So you need to know at what depth the water was found, not necessarily the depth of the well.*

Tip: *I prefer to dowse a day or so before the well is dug, but that isn't always possible. It is recommended that the well be dug at least within 6 months of dowsing the well. Plus, the sooner the well is dug after dowsing, the more likely people are to call you back with the results.*

It is best if the landowner has an understanding with the well drilling company before they even come to the property to drill. They need to be informed that the site was dowsed; that you are expecting the well at a specific site, and the depth projected. If they don't agree to this, find another well driller.

Even after arriving at this understanding, it is important the landowner be present when the well is dug because it is unlikely the drilling company will drill where you requested if you are not there. Plus, the landowner needs to be specific about the well driller slowing down when they come to the depth the dowser projected. With the high speed drilling rigs they have today, it is very easy for them to go right through a water vein and actually seal it off, never even knowing that they hit water.

In one case I know of, the landowner was present when the drilling was going on, but the driller would not stop when they found water at the depth the dowser (me) had projected. The driller said that it couldn't possibly be a good well and enough water since the other people in the area all had wells several hundred feet deeper. The driller would not even listen to the landowner since the site had been dowsed.

The landowner had not anticipated the problem (even though I had warned him) because "the man's father, the retired well driller, hadn't been like that!" Don't expect the same type of performance just because the well drilling business has passed down from generation to generation.

Tip: *Have things perfectly clear before you start drilling your well. Get a commitment in writing if you can. It's your money that is being spent to drill the well.*

In another case a well was dowsed and the driller had been informed as to where to drill. However, when the landowner came home from work, he found that the well was in a totally different place and was many hundreds of feet deeper than had been dowsed. The well cost him many thousands of dollars more than it needed to.

Years ago I was dowsing a well for a neighbor who had a friend from Texas visiting. This lady visited almost every summer but this was the first time I had met her. I had just arrived and started dowsing; she took one look at me and went inside the house. I didn't think anything of it, and it was fine with me because I prefer to not have an audience around when I dowse for water. I found the stream, staked out the stream, and marked the best spot to drill, went home and didn't think any

more about it. A couple of summers later I was visiting the neighbor and met their friend from Texas.

It was then she explained to me that when she saw me dowsing she thought I was evil, a witch or something bad, because the preacher in her church said to stay away from people who are dowsers or diviners because the Bible, according to his interpretation, says we are bad/evil people. Since then she has changed her mind about me, because after she met me she could tell that I was not an evil person. Now, I believe in the Bible, but I also believe that people can twist the Bible around to prove whatever point it is that they want to prove.

The truth is, all gifts can be used for good or all gifts can be used for evil. If I exploited this talent or "gift from God", as I prefer to call it, that would be evil. But, I don't charge outrageous prices to dowse a well, do muscle testing, or any other type of dowsing that people pay me to do. My fees are very minimal and I do the work for the greatest good of all concerned.

I feel that this is important in keeping integrity in the field of dowsing. Just know that when you do this type of work and use "unusual" skills and "strange" instruments, you may run into some misinformed people who will look at you oddly, or call you some not-too-nice names. They, luckily, are few and far between. For the most part people are very amazed that you can do such things and are able to find out such information.

But, there are good stories too—gosh, there are many good stories. Back in 2000 I dowsed a well for a handicapped lady. If anyone needed to save on the cost of drilling a well, she did. I found 2 streams on the property but I just felt that there was a better one. I found the third one and it was, oh yes, a little over 100 feet from the existing septic system. (It needed to be 100 feet away in order for them to drill according to code.) I knew this would be a good well. The pull was excellent and the water quality was good also. Most of the wells in the area both above and below her land (she was on a steep hillside) came in at a 350 to 400 foot depth. I estimated the well I dowsed on her property would be 180 to 190 feet.

They drilled a few days later and hit an artesian well. They drilled to 130 feet and the water came bursting through. The water pressure was so strong that the initial flow was 25 gallons per minute, and it almost washed her driveway out. When the well finally settled down, the water came to about 15 feet from the surface, and so she only needed to put in a shallow well pump.

I think that the reason I was off is because the water was actually deeper, but when they got to 130 feet the water pressure was so strong that it broke though before the drill hit the water level. The driller was amazed. He had never heard of an artesian in that area. The depth difference between her well and other wells in the area was between 220 feet to 270 feet, and at a drilling cost at that time of $33.00 a foot, the lady saved between

$7,000.00 to $9,000.00. She also said that the water tasted delicious.

In another case, I dowsed for a person whose property was on quite the hillside and found a stream that was not nearly as deep as the other wells in the area. She had the well drilled a few weeks later. I did not hear back directly from her but from a mutual friend who said she got the goose bumps when she found out that I was only 1 foot off in my projection of the well depth from what the actual depth was when drilled.

In another good case scenario, my first husband, Asa, dowsed a well for someone who later became a very good friend. They set up stakes mapping out the flow of the stream and the best place to drill. This is another instance of a person's property being on a steep hillside. Needing to clear out and level land for parking in front of the house, they had to do a lot of dirt moving with a big dozer.

They had tagged some trees to give an idea of where the water vein was but had lost the actual stakes during the work with the dozer. So, a few weeks later she called again wanting Asa to come and dowse so that a new stake could be set in the ground. (When you are looking at thousands of dollars for drilling a well, you want an exact spot, not just an estimated sighting down some trees.) Asa was not available but I informed her that I would be free very late that evening, about 10 P.M. I could come over then if this would work for her.

She was so amazed to find another family member that could dowse that she blurted out, "You can dowse too? You're a family of dowsers?" I informed Ruth that I had taught Asa how to dowse. Well, what a concept, a family of dowsers! I got directions and drove over later that evening.

I had no idea where the first vein had been found, and since I become very focused and tunnel visioned when doing this work, I did not notice any markings on any trees in the area. I just did my thing and found water within a few minutes. She was delighted to see that I found the same vein in the area that Asa had found it, and that I was able to immediately walk to the very spot.

She then showed me where she had tagged the trees. They were some distance away but sighting down these you could see it was on the same line. But, I can understand her wanting to have this rechecked, since the original stakes had to be moved. When you are dealing with something as expensive as putting in a well, you want to be exact. She has often mentioned in a joking manner, "Drink the water, it tastes so good. I had a good dowser!"

Don't think that water is the only thing that can be dowsed! How about dowsing for something just as valuable? Gold? Silver? Minerals? Oil? Gems?

Although I lived 35 years in Fairbanks, Alaska, I personally never had an opportunity to dowse for gold, but I know that Alaska is a mother lode of gold deposits from Nome to Fox to Central to numerous other spots around the state. I've been told that quite a number of gold miners dowse for gold deposits on their stake of land. Why not? It makes sense to me, especially since mining is such an expensive proposition, and for many small-time miners the season is very short.

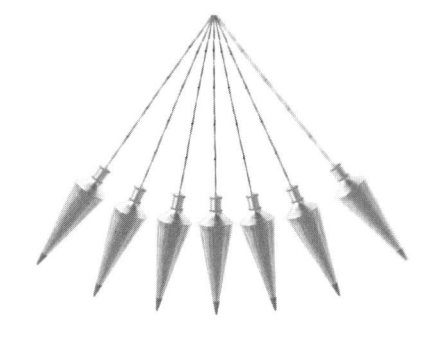

Chapter 9

Map Dowsing and Layered Water Veins

There is yet another method of water dowsing I will mention here. This method is known as **Map Dowsing.** Map dowsing is best done with a topography map, but it can also be done with a hand drawn map. The hand drawn map should be drawn to scale with the house, driveway, and all outbuildings drawn in; north, south, east, and west indicated, and the amount of acreage should be noted.

When I map dowse, I hold the pendulum in my left hand (this is the one and only time I do this because I am right-handed, and working with my left hand feels awkward). I hold a pencil in my right hand with the map on a flat surface in front of me. I slowly move the pencil along the outline of the map. I start in the upper left hand corner of the map and move to the right.

When I find a water vein, the pendulum will start moving. I make a small pencil mark to indicate this spot. After I go over the whole top border, I move down a small amount, about an inch (although this depends on the size of the map). When the water vein is again found, I make another pencil mark on the map. I continue this procedure until the markings show the flow of the stream across the land.

If you would like to work with this method, here are some tips I have found useful: If no water vein indications appear as you move across the top of the map you will need to go down the left hand side of the map. Again, make a pencil mark on the map when the pendulum spins as an indication of water. Then you will need to move in about an inch (again, depending on the size of the map) and repeat the procedure. You may find more than one water vein when you dowse in this manner.

Map out your vein or veins, and when you are finished you can connect the dots. This will give you the flow of the underground stream in relation to all of the buildings on the map and also the driveway. You can then note the best place to drill.

The first time I had an opportunity to map dowse was when visiting in Missouri. I was at my parent's home and a cousin dropped by. He mentioned that he needed to drill a well for his home. My dad told him that I was a dowser, and he was immediately interested in having me dowse a well for him. I mentioned that the water could be map dowsed, though I had never done this before, I had only seen it done. Well, this he had to see!

My mom produced the back of an envelope for Kenny to draw his property, house, and driveway. I also had him label the north, south, east, and west directions. Then I got out my pendulum and proceeded to dowse just the way I described to you. I found two streams on the property that would work well for his needs. Within the next day or two, we were able to go to his property, and we (both dad and I) dowsed out the water situation. Oddly enough, I found 4 or 5 water veins on the property, but the two very best were the two that showed up when I map dowsed.

Another opportunity for map dowsing came through the mail. I received a letter from mom and dad. In it was a hand drawn map of one of their neighbor's home and property. This map was definitely not drawn to scale—it indicated that they owned 5 acres, and according to what they had drawn, the house would have been the size of the Taj Mahal.

I called home so that I could clarify some details and get a more accurate picture of the land, home, driveway, and out buildings on the property. After I had a map that was better to scale, I did the map dowsing. I found only one water vein on the property, and it ran at an angle across the property and at an angle under the house. Because of the location of the driveway and septic system, the best place to drill the well was about 10 feet from the house at the back and side corner.

I mailed the map back to my parents (they don't have a fax) and by the time they got it back, the well driller had come and gone. Guess where the driller had put the well? About 10 feet from the back and side corner of the house, just where I had found the water vein.

Layered water veins

Luckily we never stop learning when it comes to dowsing. As I was finishing writing this book, I discovered some new information that still has me pondering the possibilities. In all the years of dowsing for water, I have never heard it taught or even spoken about, yet in retrospect it seems like one of those "Aha!" moments—one of those moments when you think, "Of course this is how it is; why didn't I think of it sooner?"

The concept is **layered water veins**. For instance, when you dowse for water you may find a vein at 150 feet, another at 210 feet, and yet another at 315 feet—one under the other. Thinking about it, this is such a likely possibility, I can't believe I didn't realize it many years ago.

You will remember that I mentioned previously that it is a good idea to be present when your well is being dowsed or, in many cases, the well driller will go right through the vein that was present at 120 feet and proceed to drill for another 100 feet before he finds what he considers a good enough vein—and stops. Obviously, he would not have been able to find water at a lower level, if another water vein had not been present under the shallower vein the dowser had found and marked.

Often when we are dowsing for someone, they are paying us to find the best stream of water at the closest depth possible, so that they can keep down the cost of drilling the well. Therefore, I have never before found it necessary to think of looking deeper and dowsing for a second, even a third vein, running underneath the vein I have just found at the most cost effective depth.

And the reason I never found these other, deeper veins is because I did not ask! When I am on the property dowsing for water or dowsing by map, I will ask for the water vein to be not below 150 feet, or 200 feet, or 250 feet, depending on the area. That is why I never found the additional water veins!

When I was in Missouri in late 2006, my cousin, Henry requested me to dowse a well for him; he was going to put in a well in the next few weeks. He knew just where he wanted the well to be, and like most people he was mainly concerned about convenience. He wanted the well to be convenient to the numerous fields where his cattle would be watered and convenient for future structures that might be built on the property. Yet he wanted the well head to be out of the way of farm equipment and not to become an obstacle. His third consideration was that the well drilling equipment would be able to get into the area easily.

He had picked out the spot. As far as he knew, this was all that was necessary, as a close neighbor had found really good water at 240 feet, so why shouldn't he? Well, the answer was clear to me when I dowsed the property: There was no water in the spot he had chosen. Oh, he was only 5 or 6 feet off, but that becomes a "miss" when there is no water vein there! I found good water at 140 feet, though there wasn't a whole lot of water in that vein.

Now, since quantity was even more important than quality in this case, he wanted me to keep looking. This was a project that was to be partly sponsored by the Government, since it had to do with a field rotation study, so the cost of drilling the well was not as important as being able to have access to the necessary quantity of water.

So, I changed my parameters. I stated that I wanted a greater quantity of water and lowered the depth. To my amazement, I found a second stream of water running directly under the first, about 100 feet deeper and about 2 feet wider. We staked both of these streams and indicated the best place to drill so that they could both be hit if need be, and so that the well head would be out of the way of cattle and farm equipment.

Four weeks later the driller came and this is what transpired. They found a small flow of water between 130 and 150 feet (I had found it at 140 feet). This was not enough for Henry's purpose. They kept drilling and found 40-50 gallons per minute at 240 feet (I had found the water at exactly 240 feet), but the water had sand in it. (Also, in Missouri, when putting in a well, the regulations read that the well must go through 40 feet of clay or solid rock, and from what I deduced from this drilling experience, limestone is not considered solid rock.)

So the well driller went down another 40 feet, through the solid rock. At 280 feet they now got over 60 gallons of clear, pure water per minute. And the water comes to 90 feet from the surface because there is so much pressure down there.

Since everybody in the area knows or is related to everybody else, one of the neighbors knew about me dowsing the well for Henry. They wanted to know what I had found concerning his prospects for a well. I told them about the depth of the first vein, and then about the second water vein I had found directly under the first but 100 feet deeper. They wanted to know if the vein that I had found for their daughter's home had a second vein under it, too.

Well, low and behold, it did! But this vein did not run exactly under the first, but at a slight angle and 60 feet deeper. We staked them both and marked the spot that the well was to be placed. Now, I placed the drilling spot not in the dead center of the first vein, but a little bit over, so that the drilling spot would hit both veins. I know the well has been dug and they found water in the spot I indicated. Beyond that, I do not currently have the information regarding depth and gpm (gallons per minute).

Knowing the information about layered veins will alter the way I now dowse for water wells and select the parameters I set. The more information a dowser can get, the better the odds for an affordable, good, clean source of drinking water.

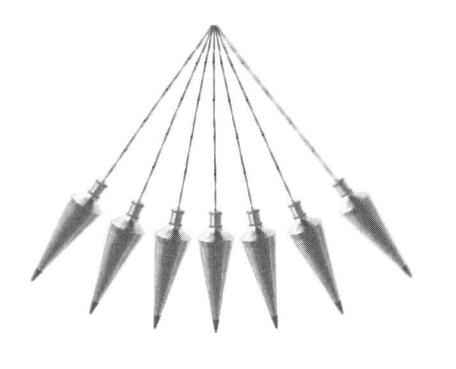

Chapter 10

Dowsing Chakras and Auras

Another area of energy work is checking one's chakras and aura layers. As I explained at the beginning of this book, we have 7 main chakras. If they are functioning properly, these chakras spin in a clockwise direction. The dowser can hold a single L-Rod over the area of the chakra, and the L-Rod will spin in the direction that the chakra energy is flowing. In this way one can check both the front and back of the body. The person whose chakras are being studied should be laying down on their back while the front chakras are checked, and on their stomach when the chakras are checked in the back.

A pendulum will work just as well as the L-Rod for checking the energy flow of the chakras. The pendulum will spin in the direction that the energy is flowing. In fact, the pendulum has one distinct advantage over the L-Rod, as the pendulum will be able to show you how open the chakra is.

If the energy from one or more chakras is barely open, the pendulum will have a very narrow swing—if any at all. After having someone who is familiar with energy work and the flow of the chakras work on the person, the dowser can once again check the flow of energy and will likely see that the pendulum is now circling with a very wide swing, moving in a clockwise direction. If the chakras are checked with an L-Rod, one is only able to detect that the clockwise direction is now the direction of the energy flow.

At the beginning of the book I spoke about our auras and mentioned that we have seven layers of auras surrounding our body. People who are very sensitive and attuned to energy work are able to feel these auric energy levels and they can tell, or rather feel, how far each level extends out and where it ends. These people are usually only able to find the first two or three levels of the aura because the energy shift becomes more subtle the further out the auric energy layers extend.

Don't be too alarmed if you are unable to sense your own energy levels or your auric fields. Only a very few people have this ability. So do not imagine that you need to worry about someone every day wandering into your energy zones and saying, "Oops, looks like Esmeralda's energy isn't going out too far today." No, at this time not too many people have the innate ability to sense these things. But by using an L-Rod, most of us have the ability to learn how to check a person's auric energy level.

Such a test is best done outside, in a park or field so that you can have a long distance to play with if you want to check all seven levels. Have the person being tested stand in one spot. Start by testing them from about 20 feet away. You only need one L-Rod for this.

I'm right handed so I hold my L-Rod in my right hand; use the hand that is most comfortable for you. Slowly walk towards the person. As you do so, the L-Rod will swing to a right angle when you encounter the outer edge of one of their seven auric layers.

The first level extends about 1 inch out from most people's bodies, though I have known some extraordinary people who, when they are teaching or projecting great amounts of energy, have the first layer extend out three inches. This first level is white and people can be trained to see it.

The second layer goes out several feet; this layer has colors in it. It is this layer that people who read auras are able to see, and they can access tremendous information about our health as well as our mental, emotional, and spiritual well being. I cannot see auras but I can feel the energy that is put out at this level. It is at this level that we can feel if a person is mad, angry, unhappy, creepy, and all those many other emotions.

You may be very surprised to find that you sense auras as well, but did not realize that this was the energy being projected from the second layer of the aura. There are five more levels to the aura, and these can extend from a foot or two outside the physical body, to miles outside of it.

As you are locating the energy layers, just keep walking further and further away from the person and then turn around and slowly walk back, towards the person, with the L-Rod held in one hand. Every time the L-Rod swings to a right angle, keep count—that is another auric energy level. Soon you will have an idea of how far the person's aura extends. The levels seem to expand exponentially, though I have not kept detailed enough information to know if it is on a phi ratio.

You may even wonder why knowing something like how far one's aura extends is even important. My feeling is that we are living in a very uncertain world. Power struggles are taking place everywhere—from those that occur between spouses to those that affect nations. Many countries have the ability to attack and destroy a part of our planet. These evil influences are everywhere: they are projecting their dark energy in to the world. We need to extend our light, bright, clear energy to counterbalance and reclaim a positive influence.

If we, as individuals want to make a difference, one way that we can do this is by spreading our positive auric influence as widely as possible. I know that there are many energy workers who feel differently; they keep their aura in as tight and close to their body as they can. I happen to feel the opposite. I think that we should be spreading light and love as much as possible! And one way of doing this is by keeping a very clean, bright aura and allowing it to flow out from us.

We can do this by practicing slow, deliberate breathing. As we breathe, we need to feel the energy in our body, then feel the energy extend out from us. This is best done when we are in a quiet, meditative space. It takes practice and it takes awareness to be able to accomplish this. We may be only able to do this breathing and awareness for short periods of time at first; sometimes our exercise may last only for seconds or minutes at a time. But with practice it will happen more easily, more often, and for longer periods.

On a personal level, when we find that we are able to achieve and maintain this calm zone, our dowsing work is easier and the results more accurate, because it is this same type of awareness/consciousness we use or access when dowsing. I find that the more I live in this state of awareness, the happier I am, and the happier my home environment is! This is a space of peacefulness—a peace of mind I wish for all of you.

After all is said and done, there really is a lot to this dowsing business. There are numerous methods and several different tools to learn to use, as well as learning to body-pendulum test. All of this takes the right tools, time, practice, and confidence in yourself.

Sometimes we need more than a great book—we need a great teacher.

I have been on a fabulous journey these past 30 plus years, both as a result of learning and of sharing this information. Each of us has been blessed with so many gifts and talents, if we could but realize them.

I hope that I have been able to give you a glimpse into my world, and to open the door to the wonderful experience of learning to use this energy, these tools and this talent. We can all benefit from sharing them with one another, and we can all be blessed if only we try.

Please contact me if you need help or if group training is needed. If it is in my power, I will do my best to help you.

Blessings from me and our Creator.

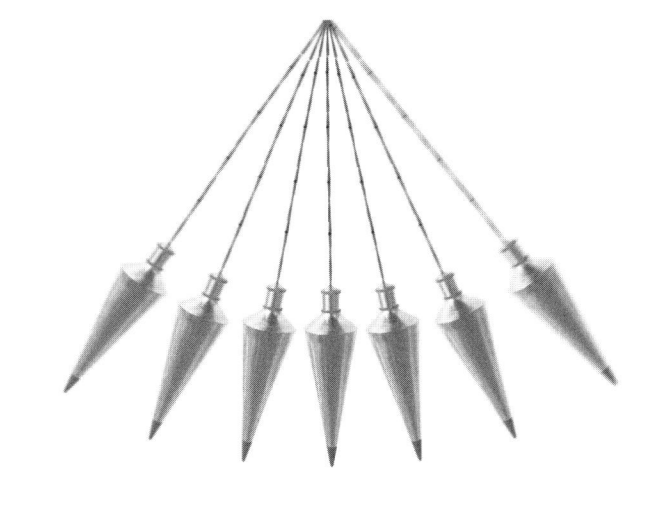

Pendulum, L-Rod, Y-Rod

Index

Symbols

R

S

W

Y

Additional Resources

Ozark Research Institute 221 S. Locust Ave., Fayetteville, Arkansas 72701
Phone: (479) 582-9197   Website: www.ozarkresearch.org

American Society of Dowsers P.O. Box 24 Danville, Vermont 05828
Phone: 802-684-3417   Website: www.dowsers.org

Dr Christopher's School of Natural Healing
Phone: 1-800-372-8255   Website: schoolofnaturalhealing.com

Walter Woods, author of *Letter To Robin—A Mini-Course in Pendulum Dowsing* and
Companion to Letter To Robin—Learning to Dowse - Student Guide and Teachers' Syllabus
(Copies can be purchased from The American Society of Dowsers Bookstore, Phone: 1-800-711-9497)

Raymon Grace, writer, dowser, lecturer and producer of instructional DVDs
Website: www.lifeenrichmentseminars.com/Raymon/index.htm

Barbara Dowdy-Trabke

About Author Barbara Dowdy-Trabke

As a youngster growing up on a farm in Southeast Missouri, Barbara's view of life suddenly expanded when she moved to Fairbanks, Alaska as a young bride. She arrived just in time to experience the history-making saga of the Alaskan pipeline and while her husband was away working on the project for months at a time, the young bride soon became familiar with the hardiness needed to endure the long, cold, snowy winters. Harsh weather and living conditions influenced Barbara's character, self-sufficient life style and indomitable spirit.

Raising four children, she managed to work and also continue her education. While the children were growing Barbara eventually recognized that the health care they were receiving was not helping them to stay healthy and prevent diseases, merely providing a pharmaceutical solution after someone was sick. She began studying herbal medicine and was soon holding weekly meetings so that others could benefit from the things she was learning. Seeking to learn more, she pursued her studies, becoming a Certified Master Herbalist, Iridologist, Reflexologist, MRM Technician and Reiki Master. For more than a dozen years Barbara has been hosting a healing circle both in Fairbanks, Alaska, and in Reno, Nevada. These circles are a time of spiritual learning, sharing and development for all who participate in them. And, she continues to share what she has learned both with her community and by traveling around the United States holding seminars and teaching others.

Barbara began dowsing when in her 20's and, over time, dowsing has not only become a way of life for her personally, but also an opportunity for great learning and sharing of the gifts she has received. Over the years in Fairbanks, Alaska, Barbara came to realize that a person was not just a body with a soul, but was more accurately, a soul with a body. Therefore body, mind and soul were all of importance. She started building on the knowledge that was sparked back in the mid-70's when she held that first forked tree twig and learned that she could dowse for water. Barbara attended Ozark Research Institute and became a member of the Fairbanks Dowsing Society and later a member of the American Society of Dowsers. Barbara has not only dowsed many water wells but she has taught individuals and classes in the techniques of dowsing and on pendulum usage.

After the death of her youngest daughter, Heather, who was killed by a drunk driver, Barbara's life changed in a myriad of ways. The connection with the spiritual strengthened. Now remarried and at home in Reno, Nevada, Barbara continues to offer alternative health and healing information for those who seek her services. She has expanded her skill, learning to read Tarot Cards and use Angel Cards along with using the pendulum (dowsing), to ascertain information that would not otherwise be available. For more than 10 years Barbara published a quarterly herbal newsletter and now, with her first book, she has found a new way of helping others who are in need of this knowledge. Barbara enjoys helping others journey along their own spiritual paths, and teaches classes on many aspects of mind/body/spirit healing, as well as giving individual readings. Artistic, creative, and an avid quilter, Barbara enjoys teaching quilting classes and making art quilts for sale—often using her own hand-dyed fabric. Recently, the international quilt scene has been enriched by several of Barbara's quilts showing both in Nashville, TN as well as Paducah, KY.

rachelle dowdy

rachelle dowdy

rachelledowdy@hotmail.com

p.o. box 404 Ester, Alaska 99725

907 479 2201

Bio-

The illustrations in this book were created by Artist Rachelle Dowdy. She was born in Fairbanks, Alaska in 1971; and in 1996 she received a B.F.A in sculpture, with a minor in painting, from the University of Alaska, Fairbanks. She is one of the co-founders of SoNot, a coalition of six visual artists who meet weekly to talk about art issues and critique one another's work. The Artists also organized *One Night Art Stands* exhibitions, set in alternative venues that happens one night only. Their final project is to curate *Double XX*, the first comprehensive look at contemporary women artists in Alaska. Dowdy's artwork consists primarily of human and animal images, combining natural materials such as wood and fibers with industrial and recycled materials. Dowdy was the recipient of a *Rasmuson Fellowship* in 2006, and a *Marie Walsh Sharpe Art Foundation Scholar* in 1989. She has worked as an artist-in-residence at *Denali National Park, University of Alaska Fairbanks, Fairbanks School District* and for the *Fairbanks Arts Association*. She has also taught sculpture classes at the *University of Alaska, Fairbanks*. She has had solo exhibitions, including at the *International Gallery of Contemporary Art, Decker/Morris Gallery, Alaska Pacific University*, and *The Center of Contemporary Art* in Anchorage; the *Bunnell Street Gallery* in Homer, *Well Street Gallery, Fairbanks Arts Association*, and the *University of Alaska Fairbanks* in Fairbanks. She has also participated in numerous group exhibitions, including the *Anchorage Museum of History and Art*, the *University of Alaska Fairbanks, Fairbanks Arts Assoc., Well St. Art Co., International Gallery of Contemporary Art, Decker/Morris Gallery, Out North Gallery, Bunnell St. Gallery, The Annex*, and the *Center for Contemporary Art*. Dowdy's work is held in many public and private collections including the *1% for Art Program, Alaska Psychiatric Institute, Anchorage Museum of History and Art, City of Anchorage, Julie Decker and Micheal Morris, Wanda Semester and Mark Fryer, Sonya Kelliher-Combs, Jocelyn Young and Asia Freeman*. Dowdy completed a private commission from the *WILD Foundation*, four life sized ferro-concrete sculptures titled *Wilderness, Wildlands and People; A Partnership for the Public*, which was installed in downtown Anchorage and gifted to the City of Anchorage and the people of Alaska. Dowdy currently lives and works in Fairbanks.

Visit www.dowsingdame.com for additional information and to choose from our selection of the items mentioned in this book.

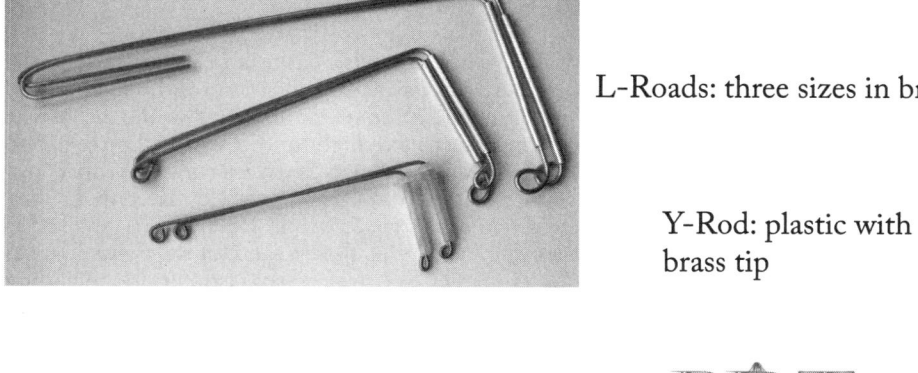

L-Roads: three sizes in brass with brass or plastic sleeve

Y-Rod: plastic with brass tip

Also Available:
Three double-sided, laminated
charts which will contain all
six charts shown in the book!